Instructor's Manual to Accompany

REPORTING FOR THE
MEDIA

Seventh Edition

FRED FEDLER
University of Central Florida

JOHN R. BENDER
University of Nebraska-Lincoln

LUCINDA DAVENPORT
Michigan State University

MICHAEL W. DRAGER
Indiana University of Pennsylvania

New York   Oxford
OXFORD UNIVERSITY PRESS

Oxford University Press

Oxford   New York
Auckland Bangkok Buenos Aires Cape Town Chennai
Dar es Salaam Delhi Hong Kong Istanbul Karachi Kolkata
Kuala Lumpur Madrid Melbourne Mexico City Mumbai Nairobi
São Paulo Shanghai Taipei Tokyo Toronto

Published by Oxford University Press, Inc.
198 Madison Avenue, New York, New York 10016
www.oup.com

Oxford is a registered trademark of Oxford University Press

Photo credit: Digital Vision Ltd.

ISBN: 0-19-516535-7

Printing number: 9 8 7 6 5 4 3 2

Printed in the United States of America
on acid-free paper

TABLE OF CONTENTS

SPECIAL FEATURES IN THIS BOOK AND MANUAL

The seventh edition of "Reporting for the Media" and this manual contain several features designed to help your students become better writers. The features include:

ANSWER KEYS

If your students would like some additional practice after reading several of the chapters and working on their exercises, they can complete the extra exercises marked "Answer Key Provided," then correct their own work. The answers to those exercises appear in the textbook's Appendix D.

APPENDICES

As in previous editions, "Reporting For The Media" provides five appendices: (1) a city directory, (2) a summary of The Associated Press Stylebook And Libel Manual, (3) rules for forming possessives, (4) answer keys and (5) common writing errors.

The names of some of the people described in the exercises are deliberately misspelled, and the city directory provides the correct spellings. This feature forces students to develop the habit of verifying the spelling of every name. In addition, some people mentioned in the exercises are prominent individuals, and only the students who use the city directory will learn their identities and be able to include that information in their stories.

The second appendix summarizes the most commonly used rules in The Associated Press Stylebook And Libel Manual, thus providing a brief and convenient reference for students (and saving them the expense of buying the entire stylebook).

END-OF-CHAPTER MATERIALS

The end-of-chapter materials vary from chapter to chapter, but they typically include: (1) lists of readings, (2) discussion questions, (3) suggested class projects, (4) newsroom bulletins and (5) guest commentaries.

This book reprints newsroom bulletins from Joe I. Hight, managing editor of The Oklahoman, and Lucille deView, writing coach for The Orange County (Calif.) Register. The bulletins explain errors news writers make and provide additional examples of good and bad writing.

To teach your students more about feature writing, communications law, ethics and public relations, the textbook includes various sidebars and columns. Some were written by the authors of the textbook; others were written by guest columnists such as Bryan Denham of Clemson University and Dean Kazoleas of Illinois State University. Other materials come from the Society of Professional Journalists and the National Center for Victims of Crime.

HUNDREDS OF EXAMPLES

"Reporting For The Media" contains hundreds of examples, some written by students and some by professionals. While introducing a new topic or discussing an error, "Reporting For The Media" typically shows students examples of the error and how to avoid or correct it.

HUNDREDS OF EXERCISES — REALISTIC AND OFTEN GENUINE

This edition of "Reporting For The Media" also contains hundreds of exercises so that you can select the ones most appropriate for your students (and assign additional exercises to students who need more practice).

To add to their realism, many of the exercises are both new and genuine. Examples include:

●President Bill Clinton's address to the memorial service for the victims of the Oklahoma City Bombing. See Exercise 6 in Chapter 12 (Speeches and Meetings).
●President George Bush's speech announcing the war against Iraq. See Exercise 5 in Chapter 12 (Speeches and Meetings).
●The transcript of a 911 call the police in Milwaukee, Wis., received about Jeffrey Dahmer, the man who admitted murdering 17 young men. See Exercise 2 in Chapter 15 (Public Affairs Reporting).

Similarly, the exercises in Chapter 10 (Interviews) contain verbatim accounts of actual interviews conducted especially for this book. They quote a college student who attacked a robber and a woman who donated the organs of her son, who died in an accident.

Other exercises, although fictionalized, were drawn from real events ranging from accidental drownings to the arrest of a horse rider for driving while intoxicated.

Plus Exercises that Contain an Ethical Dilemma

Many of the exercises contain ethical problems: four-letter words, the names of rape victims, bloody details and other material that many editors would be reluctant to publish. A list of all those exercises appears in Section IV of this manual.

Plus Exercises that Contain Sexist Remarks

Several of the exercises contain words that exclude women: fire*man*, mail*man* and police*man*, for example. Other exercises refer to women primarily as wives or seem to express surprise when they do well. A list of all the exercises that contain sexist comments appears in Section V of this manual.

Plus Exercises that Can Be Localized

Some of the exercises may mention your school, city or state. If you assign one of those exercises, you can expect your students to localize it. A list of all the exercises that can be localized appears in Section VI of this manual.

PRO CHALLENGE

Several of the exercises in the introductory chapters about writing leads and about the body of news stories are titled "Pro Challenge." Professionals were asked to complete the same exercises, and their work appears in this manual.

After asking your students to complete those exercises, you can duplicate the professionals' work and show it to your students. Your students, then, can compare their work to the professionals'.

REORGANIZED CHAPTERS

Two chapters have been added to this edition of "Reporting for the Media." All other chapters have been extensively revised. In addition, faculty members using this book suggested that several chapters be rearranged.

New with this edition are Chapter 2, Grammar and Spelling, and Chapter 16, Understandinga and Using the Internet. The Grammar and Spelling chapter introduces basic concepts in writing that will be used throughout the book, and the chapter on the Internet describes how the Internet is organized and how journalists can use it efficiently.

The chapters on The Language of News (4), The Body of a News Story (8), Interviews (10) and The News Media and the PR Practitioner (19) have been extensively revised.

The chapters also have been reorganized to better reflect the order in which instructors tend to use the material. Chapters 1 through 10 introduce skills basic to all news reporting and writing. Chapters 11 through 19 deal with more specialized or advanced types of writing. And the final three chapters discuss law, ethics and careers.

SAMPLE STORIES

After discussing a particular type of story (obituaries, for example), this book reprints entire stories written by prize-winning professionals. Students can use the professionals' stories as models for their own work.

Examples from The Associated Press, Reuters, the St. Petersburg (Fla.) Times, the Norfolk (Va.) Virginian-Pilot and the Daily Nebraskan illustrate different ways of organizing news stories. Similarly, many journalists consider Jim Nicholson of the Philadelphia Daily News the nation's best obituary writer, and some of his advice appears in Chapter 11 (Writing Obituaries).

COMPUTER SOFTWARE

Faculty members with access to Macintosh computers can use this book with "Media Writer: Computerized Lessons in News Reporting," also written by Fred Fedler of the University of Central Florida and Lucinda Davenport of Michigan State University. Like this book, the software is marketed by Harcourt College Publishers.

The software is sold separately and provides 32 interactive exercises for the students in reporting classes. The first exercises emphasize the fundamentals of newswriting: spelling, style, accuracy and objectivity. The following exercises teach students how to write more clearly and concisely. Later exercises ask students to write leads and complete news stories. The exercises also test students' news judgment — and their decisions when confronted by an ethical dilemma.

THE BEGINNING CLASS IN REPORTING AND WRITING

Journalism is an art rather than a science, and there is seldom one right way to write a story or to teach newswriting. Consequently, the ideas presented in this manual should be regarded as guidelines rather than as rigid rules. Similarly, the manual's examples should be regarded as models rather than as the only possible answers.

The textbook and instructor's manual also reflect the belief that students learn to write by writing. They should have as much writing practice as possible. Most of their writing assignments will involve news stories. Some, however, may involve abstracts, résumés or book reports.

In addition, assignments should be as realistic as possible. Thus, many of the assignments in this book are genuine: actual laws, interviews, speeches, police reports and news releases. Moreover, the exercises are intentionally disorganized and poorly worded so that students must organize the material and reword it, just as professional reporters must.

As part of this book's emphasis upon realism, some of the assignments suggested in the sample course outline (and elsewhere in this manual) require students to leave their classrooms in order to gather information firsthand. Then, to help students obtain their first clips, you can ask them to turn in two copies of those assignments: one to be graded and one to be submitted to their campus or community paper.

Here are some issues the teacher of a reporting class should consider:

GRADING

Teachers can use either a numerical or a letter system for grading newswriting assignments. A teacher using the numerical system might assign each story a maximum of 100 points, then deduct a specified number of points for each error: for example, 20 points for a factual error or misspelled name, 10 points for a lead that requires rewriting or for misspelled words other than names, five points for failure to include an important fact or for an awkward sentence, and three points for a stylistic or typographical error. Students might earn extra points for exceptional leads and for effective transitions, quotations and descriptions.

The numerical grading system has these advantages:
(1) It is more objective than other systems.
(2) Students can understand readily why they received a particular grade.
(3) Teachers quickly can compute total grades and averages at the end of a term and then place the averages on a curve.

Among the numerical system's major disadvantages is its complexity, with the possibility of a long list of penalties and bonuses. Also, teachers may find it easy to deduct points for obvious errors, but difficult to award or deduct points for a story's overall merit or style. As a result, mediocre stories that contain few glaring errors may receive high scores, whereas well-written stories that contain three or four obvious errors may receive unjustly low scores.

Other teachers award letter grades to stories based on their evaluation of the overall merit of the students' work. Teachers can assign letter grades more quickly and simply than numerical grades, but letter grades tend to be more subjective and to cause more resentment among students. Unless the teacher comments extensively on a paper, students may not understand why they received a particular grade.

Teachers can eliminate some of the confusion by explaining their grading procedures on the first day of class and by writing extensive comments on every paper. The grading criteria should be explained in detail on the course outline. Here are possible criteria on which teachers may base letter grades:

A — The story is newsworthy and exceptionally well written, thorough and free of errors.
B — The story is adequate but not exceptional.
C — The story omits important facts or needs extensive editing.
D — The story is superficial and needs extensive rewriting, or it lack newsworthiness.
F — The story is confusing, incomplete or inaccurate or it contains a misspelled name, libelous statement or serious factual error.
FF — The assignment was never turned in. (It seems unfair to give a student who came to class and tried the same grade as one who skipped class or failed to turn in the assignment. Thus, some teachers will give an "F" to the student who tried but failed, and an "FF" to the student who failed even to try. Because it counts double, the "FF" also discourages unexcused absences.)

The sample syllabus in Section III of this manual contains more complete descriptions of these letter grade criteria.

As another, but more complicated approach, teachers can give split grades: one grade for writing style and another for accuracy. For example, if a story is well-written, but contains a half-dozen spelling and stylistic errors, it might receive a grade of B/F.

Because students can learn much from rewriting their work, some teachers require rewrites of all stories that do not achieve a specified level of acceptability. Teachers assign a grade on the basis of the rewritten version of the story.

Finally, teachers can enhance the objectivity of their grading by asking students to write their names on the back of every assignment. Then, teachers will not know whose papers they are grading.

ACCURACY

Because newspapers emphasize accuracy — and because inaccuracy can carry severe consequences — students must be impressed with the necessity of checking and rechecking every fact that appears in their stories.

Teachers may adopt any of a number of policies that penalize inaccurate writing:

●Require students to rewrite any story that contains a serious factual error.
●Lower the grade on inaccurate assignments by one letter — or give an automatic F.
●Require students who make a serious factual error to write a correction for the error.

Other class policies may encourage students to check for errors in grammar and spelling (including typos and possessives). Students who submit such papers may be required to write an obituary for a prominent American. The policy encourages students to proofread their stories more carefully (students are more likely to be motivated by the threat of extra work than by the threat of a low grade).

The assignment also gives students more newswriting practice. Its major disadvantage is that it generates more papers for the teacher to correct. Here are the names of some celebrities for whom students may write obituaries:

Athletes	Political Figures	Entertainers
Peggy Fleming	Fidel Castro	Johnny Carson
George Foreman	Hillary Rodham Clinton	Glenn Close
Monica Seles	Mikhail Gorbachev	Leonard Nimoy
Johnny Unitas	Christine Todd Whitman	Mary Tyler Moore
Lee Trevino	Ralph Nader	Barbra Streisand

Newspapers make a particular effort to spell names correctly. Many of the names and addresses in the textbook's exercises are deliberately misspelled. Students can learn the importance of verifying every name and address by consulting the city directory in Appendix A. The city directory also contains newsworthy information about the identities of people in the news, information not included in the exercises.

If students write stories that include the names of actual people, they should consult the reference books regularly used by newspaper reporters, particularly telephone books and city directories. If necessary, they can call the people mentioned in their stories to confirm the spelling of their names.

Before the introduction of computers, some editors required their reporters to underline or to draw a box around every name each time it appeared in a story to indicate that they had verified the name's spelling and that the name was spelled correctly (and consistently) throughout the story. Some instructors follow that policy in their classes.

Similarly, students should report only facts — not speculation. They should not be allowed to assume anything, nor to take anything for granted.

To check on students' accuracy after they have completed an out-of-class assignment, teachers might mail accuracy forms and copies of their papers to all their sources. (A sample accuracy form appears in Section III of this manual.)

Because of the media's absolute need to meet deadlines, some teachers refuse to accept late papers. Others lower the papers' grades by one letter for each school day they are late. Similarly, some teachers refuse to accept makeup assignments. In addition to impressing students with the need for promptness, such policies encourage them to attend class.

SUGGESTED CLASS POLICIES

Just as newspaper editors and publishers adopt policies for their reporters, teachers adopt policies for their students. The policies encourage consistency and professionalism in the students' work. They also eliminate some of the students' questions and problems. Here are some ideas for classroom policies:

1. Explain class policies about grading and about late or makeup assignments on the first day of class. Doing so will eliminate the confusion and resentment that sometimes arise when questions come up later during a term. Doing so will also eliminate the problem of students who miss a half-dozen assignments, then try to turn in all the assignments on the last day of class.

2. Immediately identify the newspaper that, theoretically, will publish all the stories students write. If students know to write for a particular newspaper, perhaps the local daily or a campus

newspaper, they can be expected to follow its standards regarding matters of ethics and good taste.

3. Require students to type all their stories and to compose their stories on a typewriter or computer without writing them out in longhand first. The practice of writing stories in longhand wastes too much time. Moreover, it fails to prepare students for the rigorous demands made of professionals in the field.

4. Encourage students to report in depth and detail. Tell students to assume that the newspaper they are writing for has enough space to publish every important detail. Failure to provide such a guideline will lead some students to submit stories that are unreasonably brief. Another way to encourage students to write thorough stories is to assure them they will not be penalized for including unnecessary facts, but will be penalized if they omit important facts from their stories.

5. Give students the option of submitting an extra assignment on the last day of class. Their grade on that assignment can replace their lowest grade from the regular writing assignments. The optional assignment eliminates the problem of students who miss class — some legitimately, and some not — and who want immediate makeup assignments. The optional assignment also rewards students who attend every class and turn in every assignment. Those students can use the optional assignment, not as a makeup, but to raise their lowest grade. The optional assignment also eliminates the flow of makeup assignments that cuts into a teacher's time, and it gives students an opportunity to earn grades at a time when their writing skills have reached a peak. Here are three possibilities for the optional assignment:
   A. Review one of these books:
      1. "Confessions Of An S.O.B." by Al Neuharth.
      2. "Secrecy" by Daniel Patrick Moynihan.
      3. "Breaking the News" by James Fallows.
      4. "Don't Shoot the Messenger" by Bruce W. Sanford.
   B. Shadow a public official in your city for a work day, then write a story about the experience.
   C. Conduct an in-depth interview with a campus newsmaker. Submit two copies of your story: one to be graded and one to be submitted to the campus paper. Before conducting the interview, inform your source that the story may be published.

6. Encourage students to experiment. Many students are reluctant to try anything new: an unusual lead or descriptive phrase, for example. Students fear that their grades will be lowered if they try something new and fail. One way to encourage experimentation is to tell students that they can turn in two versions of any lead or story and label one of those versions "Experimental." Grade both versions, but record only the higher of the two grades. Then, students will never be punished, only rewarded, for trying something new. Encouraging experimentation has a second benefit: The few students who write experimental leads often provide wonderful examples that can be duplicated and discussed in class. Also, the success some students experience will encourage other students to try something new.

7. Dozens of newspapers publish newsroom bulletins that discuss errors and praise good headlines, leads and stories. Some newspapers are willing to share those bulletins with journalism teachers and students. Teachers also prepare such bulletins reviewing student work on major writing assignments. Students can learn from the mistakes made by their classmates. They can also learn by comparing their work with the best leads and stories written by their classmates. In addition, the bulletins stimulate spirited discussions and will give students permanent records of the examples the teacher considers important. Students discussing one another's work often discover

problems that their teachers overlooked. Moreover, criticism and praise from classmates can reinforce the comments made by a teacher. With practice, a teacher can prepare a two-page bulletin in an hour. Section III of this manual includes a sample classroom bulletin.

8. Encourage students to publish their work, including some of their class assignments. The sample course outline suggests that students turn in two copies of several assignments, and that one copy be submitted to their campus paper.

9. The following policies reflect a common-sense approach to teaching reporting classes. Still, stating them explicitly on the first day of class lets the students know what the teacher expects from them and what they can expect from the teacher:
    A. Return each assignment during the next class period so students receive immediate feedback on their work and are prepared for their next lesson.
    B. While making each assignment, explain its relevance. Students will work harder on assignments they think are important.
    C. Establish time limits for the completion of assignments so students become acquainted with journalists' deadline pressures.
    D. Schedule a quiz on the copy-editing symbols and on the rules in The Associated Press Stylebook and Libel Manual (condensed in Appendix B) two or three weeks after the course begins. If students are not forced to study this material, they may continue to repeat the same basic errors throughout the term. Then, the teacher wastes time correcting minor mechanical errors rather than dealing with more significant problems.

SUGGESTED IN-CLASS ACTIVITIES

Checklists

Teachers may want to distribute checklists, like the one printed in Section III of this manual, to their students. After the students finish an assignment, they can use the checklist to evaluate their own work and guide the rewriting of their papers.

Class Critiques

Critiquing stories in class can help students see what works and what does not in writing news stories. In-class critiques allow students to evaluate each other's work, to look at stories as editors and not just as writers. Sometimes students are harsh critics of one another's work. They learn that their classmates — not just their teachers — think their work can be improved.

Critiques can be handled in a variety of ways. One possibility is to have students submit two extra copies of each story. The extra copies are distributed to other members of the class who critique them. The critiqued stories are returned to the author, who incorporates the criticisms when rewriting the story. The teacher should make sure that students do not know whose stories they are critiquing. The teacher must devise some system of identifying stories by letters or codes to protect the identities of the students. Also, students must understand that they may disagree with some criticisms written by their classmates but should consider the most constructive ones.

Another possibility is to project the students' stories, or parts of them, on a screen using an overhead projector, an opaque projector or a computer projector. The entire class can then discuss each story. This method also lets the instructor focus the class' attention on specific issues raised by the students' work.

Still another approach to critiquing stories is to invite a local professional to evaluate stories as they are flashed on the screen.

Descriptions

Ask one student to stand in front of the class, and ask others to write one-paragraph descriptions of the student. Emphasize the importance of using specific details, not generalities or overall impressions. Show the results to the class, either by flashing them on a screen or compiling them in a handout. Finally, instruct students to include similar descriptions in later assignments.

As a variation on this, teachers could ask students to describe, but not name, a location that would be familiar to all. Have the rest of the class try to guess the location from the description. This makes a game of the exercise, but still offers students the opportunity to learn the value of descriptive prose that incorporates specific details.

Discussions

Devote one class period to discussing media ethics, and another class period to discussing careers in journalism. Before the discussions, the instructor may ask each student to read additional material on reserve at the library. Or, students could be asked to find one article (or one chapter from a book) about the topic and to write a two-page abstract. The first 1½ pages should summarize the article or chapter. The last half-page should evaluate and comment on it. Then, each student will be able to contribute some additional information to the discussion.

The abstract ensures that every student will read the material and be prepared for the discussion. It also provides another writing assignment.

Another possible assignment would be to have students interview professionals about ethical issues they encounter on the job.

Guest Speakers

Invite a panel of three or four local editors to speak to a class or to a larger group of students. Ask the editors to describe their internship programs and to describe the assignments newly hired editors and reporters are most likely to have. The panel might also discuss résumés and cover letters. Or, invite a panel of recent graduates to describe their jobs.

Interviews

Having students interview one another makes for more realistic assignments, and such interviews often are ideal for a two-hour period.

Ask students to write a brief descriptions of their most newsworthy experiences. The instructor can use these descriptions to select one or more students for the entire class to interview. This assignment works best midway through the term, as students are unlikely to be ready for it earlier in the term.

Select a student with a relatively simple story that involves a single dramatic event. Beginning students can write short, simple stories about fires, crimes and accidents. They have more difficulty writing good stories about complex and abstract topics that involve a multitude of diverse ideas, such as a foreign student's impressions of the United States.

To make the assignment more realistic, tell students to assume that the event occurred in their community "today," and that the local paper will publish the story "tomorrow."

The students being interviewed should be told not to prepare their remarks. This guarantees the spontaneity of the interviewees' remarks and forces the rest of the class to obtain the information they need entirely by asking the right questions.

After students have interviewed two or three classmates they may be ready to interview a local news maker.

News Releases

Teachers might ask the editors at a local paper or the student paper to save unused news releases. They can critique the releases with their students. Or, duplicate the most interesting news releases and assign them to the students. Or, ask each student to select any three and to write news stories (or only the leads) about them.

Teachers and students who have access to the Internet or the World Wide Web can find corporate, governmental or interest-group news releases posted at various sites. These electronic news releases are up-to-date and can be downloaded or printed out.

Obituaries

The exercises in the textbook provide a good introduction to obituary writing. After students have completed some of the exercises, they may be ready for more realistic assignments. Teachers can divide the class into teams of two. Ask each student to interview and write an obituary for the second member of his or her team. The assignment can be due at the end of a two-hour period.

Instruct students to assume that their classmates died at home of unknown causes that morning. (Without that guidance, students will devote their obituaries to descriptions of exotic deaths. Few students want to die of anything as mundane as cancer or heart disease.)

Or teachers may instruct students to go out and, working alone, approach two or more strangers together on campus. Students should write an obituary for one of the strangers and interview the others about the "deceased" so that they can describe their subject more fully and colorfully, using quotations and descriptions to reveal the person's interests, accomplishments and personality. The exercise forces students to approach and interview strangers — something that many are reluctant to do.

Polls

Ask students to conduct an informal poll during the first half of a class period, then to return to the classroom and to write the story during the second half. Some possible questions are listed in Exercise 7 in Chapter 17 (Advanced Reporting).

Speeches

Students can be asked to write news stories about famous speeches on video tapes, audio tapes and phonograph recordings. Some teachers or journalism departments have their own files of recordings of major speeches. Teachers can start such files by recording presidential addresses, other major speeches or press conferences. The stories students write can be compared with the stories written by professionals.

Trimming

To acquaint students with the space requirements that often confront news writers, ask them to write some stories so they will be precisely five, 10 or 20 column inches long when set in type. Or, after returning a set of papers, ask students to rewrite and trim the papers, perhaps to half their original length. Students should rewrite the stories, not just delete the final paragraphs.

SUGGESTED OUT-OF-CLASS ASSIGNMENTS

Abstracts

Outside reading assignments can be turned into writing assignments by requiring students to write two- or three-page abstracts that summarize the assigned reading's content. The abstract forces students to read the material and to take good notes. The first 1½ pages should summarize the material. In the final half page, students should comment on — evaluate — the material. For example: What did they like, dislike or find most useful? Use two criteria while grading the abstracts: (1) writing style and (2) the thoroughness and thoughtfulness of the essay.

Campus Beats

Near the end of the term, assign each student a campus beat and ask each student to find two stories on the beat. If time permits, change the beats and ask students to find two stories on their new beats.

Enterprise Stories

By the end of the term, students should be prepared to write a four- to five-page enterprise story. The first part of the assignment could be the submission of three proposals (one-paragraph descriptions) for stories that they might write for the campus newspaper. Each story proposal should involve a campus issue, not an event, and students should list a minimum of five sources for each proposal. The entire class can serve as an editorial board that critiques proposals and selects or refines the most newsworthy.

Remind students to write about a new issue, not an old group or policy. Also, students should avoid topics in which they are involved. Finally, they should interview people affected by an issue and not simply the officials responsible for it.

Each student should prepare two copies of the enterprise story, one for the instructor to grade and the other to submit to the campus paper. The assignment is more realistic than most and gives students an opportunity to obtain clips.

Interviews

Ask each student to conduct an in-depth interview with a campus news maker. Each student should interview a different person on campus, and each interview should include some descriptions and direct quotations. The interviews should focus on a single issue and be a minimum of two pages long. As with the enterprise story, students might submit the stories to the campus newspaper as well as to the instructor.

Publications Review

To acquaint students with publications in the field of journalism, ask them to write a two- or three-page paper, typed and single-spaced, that compares the content of four or five major publications. Publications the students might review include: American Journalism Review, Brill's Content, Columbia Journalism Review, The Quill, Advertising Age, Broadcasting and Cable, Editor & Publisher, Presstime, Journal of Mass Media Ethics, Journalism Quarterly or Newspaper Research Journal. Instructors might assign two of the publications to be reviewed and let each student select two others. Students can then discuss the publications in class.

Real-Life Assignments

Near the end of the term, ask the editor of a small daily or weekly in the area to provide one assignment for each student. Ask the students to turn in two copies of their stories: one to be graded and one to be given to the editor and considered for publication. Instructors may want students to rewrite their stories before submitting them to the editor. The assignment is more realistic than most and, again, gives students an opportunity to obtain more clips.

Résumés

Ask your students to write their résumés and cover letters asking for internships or full-time jobs at specific publications. The assignment, especially when made near the start of a term, helps teachers learn more about their students. The assignment also gives students an opportunity to polish their résumés and cover letters before submitting them to potential employers.

Shadowing

Ask each student to shadow a reporter for a half or full day, interview the reporter at the end of the day and to write a report about the experience. Then, in class, ask the students to describe their experiences.

SECTION III

CLASS MATERIALS

SAMPLE COURSE OUTLINE
(For a 15- or 16-Week Course)

Instructor:
Office:
Office Telephone:
Office Hours:

Name of Course
Course Prefix and Number
Term and Year

Textbook: Reporting for the Media, seventh edition.

Purpose: To help students learn to use the language correctly; to be accurate; to work under and respect deadlines; and to recognize, gather and assemble news into readable form.

Prerequisites:

Schedule:

Session 1.   Introduction. Newswriting style.
Readings for week: "Preface," Chapters 1, 2 and 6, and Appendix C (Rules for Forming Possessives).

Session 2.   Exercise 1 in Chapter 1 is due at the beginning of the period. Discuss leads. For later class interviews, students will be asked to type a separate paragraph about each of their three most newsworthy experiences.

Session 3.   Leads 1-5 in Exercise 3, Chapter 6, are due at the beginning of the period. Discussion and exercise: AP style.
Readings for week: Chapters 3 and 4, Appendix B (The Associated Press Stylebook), and Appendix E (Common Writing Problems).

Session 4.   Exercise 3 in Chapter 2 is due at the beginning of the period. Discuss leads. Class exercise: Evaluating leads (Exercise 1 in Chapter 6).

Session 5.   Leads 6-10 in Exercise 3, Chapter 6, are due at the beginning of the period. Discuss news judgment: Exercise 1 in Chapter 5.
Readings for week: Chapters 7 and 8.

Session 6.   Exercise 2 in Chapter 4 is due at the beginning of the period. Discuss leads. Discuss the body of news stories.

Session 7.   Complete news story is due: the first story in Exercise 2, Chapter 8 (Pro Challenge).

Discussion: Evaluating alternative leads (Exercise 1 in Chapter 7). Also: Evaluating transitions and second paragraphs (Exercise 1 in Chapter 8). Newswriting exercise: Leads 1-6 in Exercise 4, Chapter 6 (Pro Challenge).

Session 8.   Discuss first news story and leads. Newswriting exercise.

Session 9.   Quiz: format, style, spelling and vocabulary. Class exercise: Leads 1-5 (City Beat) in Exercise 5, Chapter 6 (Pro Challenge).
Readings for week: Chapter 20.

Session 10.   Second story is due: Exercise 2, Story 2 in Chapter 8 (Pro Challenge). Discussion and exercise: libel, Exercises 1 and 2 in Chapter 20.

Session 11.   Exercise 1 in Chapter 9 is due at the beginning of the period. Discuss second story. Discussion and exercise: the use of attribution.
Readings for week: Chapter 9.

Session 12.   Third story is due. Review: attribution and libel. Newswriting exercise. (Select any exercise in Chapters 6, 7 or 8.)

Session 13.   Discuss third story. Class exercise: writing obituaries (any exercise from Chapter 11).
Readings for week: Chapters 10 and 11.

Session 14.   Quiz covering chapters 8, 9, 10, 11 and 20: true/false questions and attribution exercises. Discussion: interviewing techniques. Class interview of fellow student, using ideas provided earlier.

Session 15.   First interview is due. Newswriting exercise (any exercise from Chapter 9 or 10).
Readings for week: Chapter 12.

Session 16.   Discuss first interview. Discuss advance and follow stories. Write advance story: First part of Exercise 3 in Chapter 12.

Session 17.   Follow story is due: Second part of Exercise 3 in Chapter 12. Class interview conducted and written in class. The assignment is due at the end of the period.
Readings for week: Chapters 21 and 22.

Session 18.   Discuss follow story and class interview. Discuss "Careers" and "Ethics." (See the discussion questions at the end of Chapter 21.)

Session 19.   Class interview conducted and written in class. The assignment is due at the end of the period.

Session 20.   Guest lecture or newswriting exercise (second obituary).

Session 21.   Two copies of a story about a campus speech, meeting or other approved event are due at the beginning of the period. Class evaluation of the stories. (Flash the stories on a screen. Or have three other students edit each story, then return it to its author for rewriting.)

Session 22.   Turn in two copies of three proposals (one-paragraph descriptions) for stories you might write for the final project. Each proposal should describe a potential enterprise story (an issue or problem — not an event — on campus). Copies of your completed story will be given to the campus and/or local newspaper. Class critique of your story ideas.

While developing your ideas, consider these guidelines:
* Do not conduct a poll.
* Do not write about a topic in which you are involved.
* Do not write about an existing (old) group or program unless you find a new development.
* Do select a topic relevant to your campus and of interest to hundreds of its students.
* Do list a minimum of five first-hand sources you will use for the story.
* Do present both sides of controversial issues.
* Do interview people affected by the issue, not just the officials responsible for it.
* Do write an in-depth story: at least four or five pages.

Your grade on this assignment will count three times as much as your grades on other assignments.

Session 23.   Exercise 5 in Chapter 19 is due. Discussion and exercise: Handling news releases. Discuss Exercise 1 and complete another exercise in Chapter 19.
Readings for week: Chapter 19.

Session 24.   Campus poll or guest lecture. Conduct a poll on campus during the first half of the period. The completed story is due at the end of the period. (See Exercise 7 in Chapter 17.)

Session 25.   Newswriting exercise: An exercise from Chapter 13.
Readings for week: Chapter 13.

Session 26.   Conduct a second campus poll. Conduct a poll on campus during the first half of the period. The completed assignment is due at the end of the period.

Session 27.   Newswriting exercise: an exercise from Chapter 15 (Public Affairs Reporting).
Readings for week: Chapter 15.

Session 28.   Discuss public affairs story. Newswriting assignment: second exercise from Chapter 15.

Session 29.   Two copies of the final project are due. Class discussion and evaluation of the stories.

Session 30.   Newswriting exercise from Chapter 13 or 15. Optional story is due.

NOTE: The class schedule may be modified from time to time if, for example, a guest speaker becomes available or an event that everyone can cover on campus occurs during a class period.

Course Requirements
--Accuracy.
--Regular attendance.
--Respect for deadlines.

Format For All Stories

--Type and double-space.

--Place your name on the back of the last page.

--Use the proper copy-editing symbols to correct your errors.

--Place the slugline and date in the upper lefthand corner. Be specific (but limit the slugline to two or three words).

--To provide space for comments, begin one-third down the first page and at the top of all succeeding pages.

Other Guidelines

Complete the reading assignments before coming to the first class each week, and bring the textbook to every class. You may also find it helpful to bring a small dictionary or spelling guide.

Assume that every story you write will be published by (your local daily) the day after it is turned in. Thus, while writing your stories, consider that paper's audience, standards and time of publication.

Every reporter must learn to think and compose on a computer or typewriter and to produce clean copy with reasonable speed; therefore, you will not be permitted to compose first in longhand.

Because accuracy and promptness are essential to the media, those requirements will be emphasized in this class. Assignments completed outside of class are due at the beginning of each period. If you know in advance that you will be late or unable to attend class, turn in your assignment early. If a problem arises and you cannot meet a deadline, notify your editor (the instructor) in advance.

Stories turned in late — after papers are collected at the start of the period — will be graded down one letter. Papers turned in a school day late will be graded down a second letter. Papers turned in two days late will be graded down a third letter, etc.

As spelling is vital to your credibility, you will be penalized for misspelled words. The spelling of every name that appears in a story should be verified with a second source, usually a telephone book or the city directory in the back of the textbook. To show that you have verified a name's spelling (and that the name is spelled consistently throughout your story), draw a box around the name every time it appears in the story.

Stories that contain a serious factual error, a libelous statement, a misspelled name or three or more spelling errors (including typos) will receive an automatic "F." Students will receive a double "FF" if they do not bother to turn in a story.

All your grades will be averaged at the end of the semester to determine your final grade in the class. Grades on the final project — the enterprise story — will be weighted three times as heavily as other grades.

Optional Assignment

You may submit an optional assignment on the last day of class. Your grade on the optional assignment can replace your grade on an assignment you missed or your lowest grade on a previous writing assignment. For the optional assignment, you can:

1. Spend the day with a public official and write a story about the experience.

2. Write a critical review of any one of these books:

    A. "Confessions Of An S.O.B." by Al Neuharth.

    B. "Secrecy" by Daniel Patrick Moynihan.

    C. "Breaking the News" by James Fallows.

    D. "Don't Shoot the Messenger" by Bruce W. Sanford.

3. Conduct a second in-depth interview with a campus news maker. Turn in two copies. One will be given to the campus paper.

Experimental Option
If you would like to try something different — to experiment — without jeopardizing your grade, you can write two versions of any lead or story: your regular version and an experimental version. Label them, and I'll grade both — then record only the higher grade.

Grading Criteria
A — The story is newsworthy and exceptionally well-written: thorough and free of errors. The lead is clear, concise and interesting. Moreover, the lead emphasizes the news: the story's latest and most interesting, unusual and important details. The body is well-organized and contains effective transitions, quotations, descriptions and anecdotes. The story emphasizes the human element and quotes a variety of sources (not just one). Because of the story's obvious merit, newspapers would be eager to publish it.

B — The story is adequate but not exceptional. A newspaper could publish the story after some editing. The lead summarizes the story, and the following paragraphs are reasonably well-organized. However, the story contains a few minor errors and might be more interesting, thorough or cohesive.

C — The story omits important information or could be published only after extensive editing. The lead may be too wordy or may fail to emphasize the news. The story fails to develop the human element, tends to be disorganized and contains several minor errors. Several sentences are vague, long or complicated and use passive rather than strong verbs. The sentences may have to be rewritten because they are so awkward, wordy or confusing.

D — The story is superficial or confusing, or requires extensive rewriting. Or, the story contains an unacceptable number of style, spelling and grammatical errors. The story may also be of questionable newsworthiness.

F — The story could not be published by a paper, nor easily rewritten. It is too confusing, incomplete or inaccurate. Or, it contains a misspelled name, libelous statement or serious factual error.

FF — The assignment was never turned in.

SAMPLE CLASSROOM BULLETIN

Course Name
Term

VICTORIES & DEFEATS

Circle The Best Lead

1.   Fifty percent of the drug abusers entering treatment programs go back to using drugs. But the Elkart Treatment Center has a unique program to end the cycle, a counselor from the center said Thursday.

2.   Conflicting testimony highlighted the first day of the trial of a woman charged with battery on a law enforcement officer.

3.   A man who assaulted two police officers, resisted arrest and claims he could not understand English was sentenced Monday to five years probation.

4.   A six-member jury Thursday found a college student guilty of kidnaping a coed from a party.

Select The Better Lead In Each Group

A.   A cardiologist is being sued for medical malpractice because he failed to detect a patient's heart problem.

B.   A man who suffered a heart attack and stroke while under the care of a cardiologist sued the cardiologist Monday for medical negligence.

A.   A woman is suing North Lake Foods Inc., owners of Waffle House Restaurants, for pain, suffering and bodily and mental injuries.

B.   A woman is suing the owners of Waffle House Restaurants, charging that a waiter poured hot coffee on her lap.

A.   A 13-year-old girl told a jury Monday that her stepfather sexually abused her almost every day for two years.

B.   "My stepfather had sex with me almost every day for two years," a 13-year-old girl told a jury Monday.

Good Leads Are Specific

A couple filed suit against a service station Tuesday, claiming that its employees were negligent.

REVISED: A lawsuit filed Tuesday charges that service station employees doused a couple and the interior of their car with gasoline.

A 22-year-old man was sentenced Wednesday to five years of probation after being convicted of resisting arrest and battery on a police officer.

REVISED: A 22-year-old man was sentenced Wednesday to five years of probation after being convicted of kicking a police officer.

Too Much Comment In Lead

A small fire at a home Wednesday made the dangers of playing with fire a reality for a baby sitter and two friends.

Good Quotes

1.   Officer George Webb said he noticed Butler speeding on University Boulevard and pulled him over. "He seemed pretty belligerent at the time," Webb said. "Then, when I gave him the ticket, he hit me."

2.   In court Tuesday, Bethune said she sold crack cocaine to support her four children, ages 1, 2, 3 and 7. An aunt and a sister care for them.
        Judge Stricklan asked Bethune, "Why aren't you caring for your children?"
        In a quiet voice Bethune said: "The reason they have my kids is because I can't get my life together. They're better off where they are. Their father doesn't pay child support, and I'm just not living right."

Style Errors

        $1000 to $2000 ... teenager ... a 17 year old girl ... October 7 ... studying Journalism and French ... South Bend, Indiana ... Friday at 2:00 PM ... 815 Charles Street ... at 10 p.m. Wednesday night.

Wordy/Simplify

        relocated = moved
        were aware of = knew
        filed suit against = sued
        claimed the lives of = killed
        as a direct result of = because

Passive

        It is estimated by Alvarez that the store's debts total $340,000.
        REVISED: Alvarez estimated that the store's debts total $340,000.

        A motion was made to approve the license by Commissioner Thomas.
        REVISED: Commissioner Thomas made a motion to approve the license.

Weak Verb

        There was about $20 in the cash register.
        REVISED: The cash register contained about $20.

        Officer Robert DeSalvo did the investigation.
        REVISED: Officer Robert DeSalvo investigated.

Strong Verbs

        An armed man robbed a loan company of about $700, hopped into a waiting car and escaped before police arrived Wednesday.

Overloaded Sentence

        Jim Boudnot, 6, and his younger brothers, Matthew, 3, and Tony, 2, were asleep in their bedrooms in their home at 815 Charles Drive while their teen-age baby sitter, Lynn Biaggi, entertained two friends and was making some popcorn when the fire broke out in the kitchen at about 10 p.m.
                                                        Number of ideas in sentence_____

Needs Attribution

1.   The price seemed high.
2.   The proposal would help only wealthy investors.

Too Much Jargon

higher density rezoning ... a multi-phased project ... interest in escrow ... allows probable cause ... a forfeiture law.

Keep Related Words And Ideas Together

Dr. Sara Kaeppler said she ran <u>tests</u> on the student, a 22-year-old junior studying history at Yale, <u>which</u> revealed that he is dying of AIDS.

Spelling Errors

occured ... defendent ... sherriff ... amoung ... detremental ... medias ... licence ... recieved ... thier ... recomendation... anounced.

Clichés

lone gunman ... arrived at the scene ... fled the scene ... took off with ... opened fire ... escaped serious injury.

Too Vague

some time ago ... many homes ... a couple of months ago.

Langdon said the changes would cost a lot of money.

The city had a police dog until a year ago. The Council members said there were problems with the dog and the handler, and that two lawsuits were involved.

Other Guidelines

1. Refer to college students (and anyone 18 or older) as "men" and "women," not "boys" and "girls."
2. Mention an individual's gender, race and religion only when that information is clearly relevant to your story.
3. Begin leads with the news, not 10 or 20 words of attribution.
4. Do not use nouns as verbs: for example, "She waitressed for three years."

Grades: 2 A's, 4 B's, 7 C's, 2 D's, 1 F.

(INSTRUCTORS: If space permits, reprint the best stories written by your students. Also, give bylines to students who wrote the best leads and stories. In addition, you may want to duplicate examples of good or controversial stories published by your campus paper or local daily. Or, you can attach and discuss copies of current articles about journalism.)

STORY REVIEW
Newswriting Checklist

I. The Lead

1. Number of words in your lead:_____ (If your lead exceeds 30 words — about three typed lines — it probably requires rewriting.)

2. Number of ideas in your lead:_____

3. Is your lead a simple sentence?
        Yes_____ No, it probably requires rewriting_____

4. Is your lead likely to interest your friends?
        Yes_____ No, it probably requires rewriting_____

5. Does your lead emphasize your story's most recent, important and unusual details?
        Yes_____ No, it probably requires rewriting_____

6. Is your lead specific: so specific that readers can visualize the story?
        Yes_____ No, it probably requires rewriting_____

7. Have you avoided using any jargon or unfamiliar names in your lead?
        Yes_____ No, it probably requires rewriting_____

8. Does your lead contain a strong, active, descriptive verb?
        Yes_____ No, it probably requires rewriting_____

II. The Body

1. Have you provided a transition from your lead to your second paragraph?
        Yes_____ No, the second paragraph requires rewriting_____

2. Does the second paragraph emphasize the news — interesting or important details about the topic summarized in your lead — not background information or details about some other topic?
        Yes_____ No, the second paragraph requires rewriting_____

3. How many words are in the body's longest sentence?_____ (If the sentence exceeds 30 words, it may require rewriting.)

4. How many words are in the body's average sentence?_____ (If the average sentence exceeds 20 words, your entire story may require rewriting.)

5. What percentage of your sentences contain a weak verb: "is," "are," "was" or "were"?_____ (Circle all your story's weak verbs.)

6. List your story's strongest — most active and descriptive — verbs: _____
_____

7. What percentage of your sentences begin with a clause or phrase? _____

8. What percentage of your sentences begin with "there is," "there are," "there was," "there were" or a similar construction? _____

9. Have you used good quotations? Yes_____ No_____

10. Have you used good descriptions? Yes_____ No_____

11. Have you explained or defined every unfamiliar term?
Yes_____ No, the story requires rewriting_____

12. Have you avoided all jargon, clichés and euphemisms?
Yes_____ No, the story requires rewriting_____

13. Have you avoided sentences that would sound awkward in a casual conversation with friends?
Yes_____ No, the story requires rewriting_____

14. Have you also avoided sentences that:
   A. State the obvious?   Yes_____ No_____
   B. Report what did not happen? Yes_____ No_____
   C. Are wordy or redundant?   Yes_____ No_____

III. Finally, Have You

1. Continually emphasized the details most likely to interest your readers?
Yes_____ No_____
2. Emphasized the human element?
Yes_____ No_____
3. Used specific examples and anecdotes?
Yes_____ No_____
4. Used short, plain, familiar words?
Yes_____ No_____
5. Used the normal word order: subject, verb and direct object?
Yes_____ No_____
6. Interviewed some of the people likely to be affected by your story, not just the policy makers responsible for it?
Yes_____ No_____

ACCURACY FORM

Student Name:_____

Course:_____

Dear (Name of Source):

A college student recently interviewed you, and I would like to ask you three questions about the interview and story. Your answers will help me evaluate the story. They will also help the student improve his or her interviewing and writing techniques.

The student was told that you would be sent a copy of the story. After reading it, please answer the following questions. If you need more space, use the back of this page.

1. Is the story accurate? If not, please describe its errors.

2. Was the student a good interviewer? If not, how could the student improve his or her interviewing skills?

3. Please add any other comments you care to make regarding the student's work or approach.

For your convenience in returning this accuracy form, I am enclosing a stamped, pre-addressed envelope.

Sincerely Yours,

(Your Name and Title)

SECTION IV

EXERCISES THAT RAISE ETHICAL ISSUES

Chapter 6: Basic News Leads

Exercise 2, Section V, Lead 2.
Does anyone in your class object to the use of the word "cripple"? If so, are there suitable substitutes?

Chapter 7. Alternative Leads

Exercise 3. Lead 5.
Should reporters repeat the word "damn"? Also, should they clean up the car thief's direct quotations, correcting his grammatical errors?

Chapter 8. The Body of a News Story

Exercise 2. Story 5.
Should students quote any anonymous sources? In this case, the source is a pharmacist who "asked that she not be identified by name."

Exercise 3. Story 1.
Should the complete address of the girl be given in this case or should her parents also be identified in the story?

Exercise 3, No. 2.
Should reporters quote a source who describes a victim as almost cut in half? Or is that too gruesome for newspaper readers?

Exercise 3. Story 5.
The story uses the euphemism "senior citizens," which some people might find objectionable.

Exercise 4. Story 2 (Housing Project).
Is there a particular need to use Onn's middle name (Chinn) rather than just the middle initial? Using the name may identify the victim's race which is not necessary for the story and it takes up space.

Exercise 4. Story 3 (School Attendance Incentive Program).
Should students use the quote, "It's a hell of a mess"?

Chapter 9. Quotations and Attribution

Exercise 4. Story 1.

Is the use of the trade name "Winston" cigarettes appropriate in this story? Does it provide relevant and important information? Would the use of the name be fair to the manufacturer in this situation?

Chapter 10. Interviews and Polls

Exercise 3. Interview With a Robbery Victim.
Should reporters identify this college student? The student explains that she has not told her parents about the incident. Is her name important to the story? Or, did the student waive her right to privacy while giving the interview? Also, should students polish the source's quotations, eliminating her grammatical errors and phrases such as "you know"?

Exercise 6. Hospital Bill.
Should students use the words "damn" and "hell" in their stories? Should they polish the source's direct quotations, eliminating words such as "uh" and "ya"?

Chapter 11. Writing Obituaries

Exercise 1. Writing Obituaries
1. Veronica Dawn Blackfoot. Should the obituary mention that Blackfoot's son was adopted? Should it say that Blackfoot had been ill with breast cancer?

2. Lynn Marie Shepard. Should the obituary mention that Shepard died of symptoms caused by the use of a large quantity of cocaine? Should the obituary list Shepard's roommate among her survivors?

Exercise 2. Writing Obituaries
1. Terrance C. Austin. Is it necessary to mention Austin smoked two packs of cigarettes a day? Should the obituary identify Camels as the brand he smoked? Should the obituary quote his wife as saying smoking was the cause of his death?

2. Ann Capiello. Should reporters say before or after an autopsy that a person died of apparent suicide and from an overdose of prescription drugs? Is it important to include where the body was found and that it is awaiting an autopsy? Is her relationship with her boyfriend newsworthy? Should journalists list her boyfriend as a survivor? Should the obituary mention the daughter she gave up for adoption?

3. Kevin Barlow. Should a reporter write that a body was "donated for transplants, with remains to be cremated and scattered"? What should be mentioned about Barlow's being gay or his commitment ceremony with Bernaiche? Should journalists list Bernaiche among the survivors? Should Cortez be quoted as saying some officers were "asses" about Barlow's sexual orientation?

Chapter 12. Speeches and Meetings

Exercise 3. The Police and the Press.
The police chief tells of a college student who accidentally killed himself during autoerotic asphyxiation. Should the story include that? The police chief also describes a couple of murder cases. How much detail about the victims' deaths should the story include?

Exercise 8. School Board Meeting.
During a school board meeting, several parents debated the issue of creationism vs. evolution. One of the parents, Claire Sawyer, objected to biology books that "never mention the theory of creationism." The city directory reveals that Sawyer is a minister at Christian Redeemer Church. During the meeting,

Sawyer never mentioned her religious affiliation or position at the church. Should reporters mention it in their stories?

Exercise 9. City Council Meeting.

Should reporters clean up the speakers' direct quotations, eliminating such words as "uh" and "you know"? Should they correct the sources' grammatical errors and eliminate the profanities?

Chapter 13. Specialized Types of Stories

Exercise 5. Roundups — Multiple Sources.

Should reporters use the word "damn" while quoting a fire chief? Also, should reporters correct the sources' grammatical errors and polish their direct quotations, eliminating words such as "uh"?

Exercise 8: Sidebars.

The story quotes a sheriff who uses several profanities. Should students use any of the profanities in their stories? Why?

Chapter 14. Feature Stories

Exercise 3. Scholarship Searches.

The story quotes the Federal Trade Commission and two people who claim to have been cheated by scholarship search companies, but it does not quote any of the companies. Should their responses be included? Two companies are identified by name. Should those names be included even if the companies refuse to answer reporters' questions? Also, Al Giangelli's parents are divorced. Is this relevant?

Exercise 3. Missing People.

One of the missing people is a 14-year-old girl. Should she be identified by name? Should the story include the details of her family life? Another source is a man who tried to evade alimony and child support payments. Should his former wife be interviewed, too?

Chapter 15. Public Affairs Reporting

Exercise 1: A Child's Heroism.

A 6-year-old girl called for help while her mother was being raped. Should reporters identify the child? If they do, they will also identify her mother. Is it fair to identify the suspect but not the victim?

Exercise 2: The Dahmer Tapes.

Should students polish any of the caller's direct quotations?

Chapter 18. Writing for Broadcast

Exercise 3: second story.

Should the story refer to Pinero as J.T. or as Jim Timmons, the name that appears in the city directory?

Exercise 5: fifth story.

The story identifies one of the victims with her husband's name. The city directory notes that Tracy Aneja is a carpenter. Should students mention the "pools of blood"? Or, is that unnecessarily sensational, in poor taste and a cliché?

Chapter 20. Communication Law

Exercise 2. Libel.
Should a reporter include Williams' profanity? The reporter and the newspaper probably cannot be sued for publishing the derogatory statements Williams made during a public meeting of the city council, but do reporters and news organizations have an ethical obligation to refrain from using such statements? Should the reporter have interviewed Fong before publishing this story? What should the reporter do if Fong refused to be interviewed?

Exercise 3. Libel.
At least some of the information for this story comes from convicted felons. Should a news organization ever use such information? If so, when and with what precautions?

Exercise 4. Privacy.
Most states do not conceal the names of rape victims or forbid the publication of their names. Nevertheless, most news organizations refrain from publishing the names. Should the Weekly Intelligencer have refrained from identifying Jasmine Lynd as a rape victim?

Chapter 21. Ethics

Exercise 2: first story
A. Some people consider the term "ex con" derogatory. Should students use it in their stories?
B. Should students identify the nursing home that employs two former prostitutes?
C. Should students identify a man convicted of molesting children in 1981, and who has not been in any trouble since his release from prison in 1993?
D. Should students mention two allegations impossible to verify: allegations that some nursing homes restrained or sedated residents?
E. The story calls Rosolowski a "spokesman."

Exercise 2: second story
A. Is the students' race relevant? Should it be reported?
B. Should news stories identify both the suspects and their parents?
C. Should anyone report that a suspect's mother is divorced and on welfare, and that the suspect's father has disappeared?
D. Is it important to include that Gandolf is the widow of a city council member, and that Grauman is a local minister?

Exercise 2: third story
A. Should students report the allegations of torture? Is that in good taste?
B. Should students report the victim's criminal record? Is it relevant, or unnecessarily damaging to the victim's reputation?
C. Should students report unproven allegations that the victim: 1) belonged to a gang and 2) "was dealing drugs"?
D. Note the poor grammar and poor vocabulary used in this story. Should it be corrected?

SECTION V

EXERCISES THAT RAISE SEXISM ISSUES

Many of the book's exercises contain words that exclude women: words such as "fireman," "policeman" and "mailman." Some exercises use the words while referring solely to men. Some use the words while referring to women, and some use the words while referring to both men and women. Also, some of the words appear in paraphrases, and some in direct quotations.

At the beginning of the term, you might discuss the problem with your students and agree upon a policy that everyone will follow. Students might object to the words in some, but not every, circumstance.

Also, do the students in your class want to ban every word ending in "-man," including "freshman," "gunman" and "snowman"? If so, can they suggest acceptable substitutes for those words?

Chapter 1. The Basics: Format and AP Style

Exercise 5. No. 6.
The sentence mentions "Mrs. Richard Miehee" (misspelled as "Miehe"), using her husband's name rather than hers.

Exercise 5. No. 15.
The sentence mentions "Mrs. Samuel Swaugger" (misspelled as "Swauger"), using her husband's name rather than hers.

Exercise 6. No. 10.
The sentence calls a woman in her 20s a "girl."

Chapter 3. Newswriting Style

Exercise 2. Section VI, No. 2.
The story uses the term "gunman," implying that only men can rob banks. The term "robber" would be better.

Exercise 3.
The entire exercise: Sexism.

Exercise 4. Section V.
The entire section.

Exercise 5. Section I, No. 2.
Is it necessary to provide a physical description of the woman in the sentence?

Exercise 5. Section V, No. 6.

The sentence uses the masculine pronoun "he" while referring to a young child. A young child also could be a female.

Exercise 5. Section V, No. 9.
The woman's parentage, age and marital status may not be relevant to the story.

Exercise 5. Section V, No. 11
The father and children are named in the story, but the woman is referred to simply as "his wife." All members of the family, including the mother, should be named.

Exercise 5. Section V, No. 12.
Is a physical description of the woman necessary in the story? If not eliminate it. Also, the sentence implies that a woman can not write a book about auto mechanics.

Chapter 4. The Language of News

Exercise 5. Section I, No. 5.
A sentence refers to males as "men," but females as "ladies."

Exercise 5. Section II, No. 2.
Should reporters use the word "freshmen"? If not, what is a suitable substitute?

Chapter 6. Basic News Leads

Exercise 2. Part V, Lead 4.
Note the use of the word "repairmen."

Exercise 3. Lead 1.
Should reporters use the word "firemen"?

Exercise 4. Lead 2.
The story uses the masculine "he" while referring to the president of your school. Yet some schools, perhaps yours, have female presidents. Students at those schools should correct the error.

Exercise 4. Lead 6.
Note the use of the word "spokesman."

Exercise 5. State Beat, Lead 1.
The story calls all the editorial writers in your state "newspapermen."

Exercise 5. State Beat, Lead 2.
The story calls a woman a "spokesman."

Chapter 8. The Body of a News Story

Exercise 2. Story 6.
Although the robber has been identified as a male, should the word "gunman" be used?

Exercise 4. Story 2: Housing Project.
Should students use the word "statesmen," which appears in a direct quotation? Should students use the

word if they paraphrase the quotation?

Chapter 9. Quotations and Attribution

Exercise 1. Section IV, Sentence 8.
While attributing this sentence, students should not assume that the police officer is a man. In fact, the city directory reveals that the officer is a woman.

Exercise 1. Section IV, Sentence 9.
Note the use of the word "statesman."

Chapter 13. Specialized Types of Stories

Exercise 1. Story 4.
Note the story's use of the word "firemen."

Exercise 5, Roundups.
A man who escaped from a burning nursing home describes the "firemen" who helped rescue residents of the home. Should students change the word to "firefighters"? Does it matter whether they use the word in a direct or indirect quotation?

Exercise 6, Roundups.
This roundup story about three fires uses the words "firemen," "repairman" and "spokesman." In addition, it refers to "Mr. and Mrs. Timothy Keel" and quotes Mrs. Keel, but never uses her first name, only her husband's.

Exercise 7.
This story repeatedly uses the words "men" and "fireman."

Chapter 15. Public Affairs Reporting

Exercise 3, first report.
Students should not assume the reporting officer is a man; "S. Cullinan" stands for "Susan Cullinan," a sheriff's deputy.

Exercise 5, second report.
Students should not assume the supervising officer is a man; "T. Dow" stands for "Tammy Dow," a police sergeant.

Exercise 6, first report.
The report refers to Mr. and Mrs. Michael Deacosti and does not use Peggy Deacosti's first name.

Chapter 18. Writing for Broadcast

Exercise 5, fourth story.
This story uses the word "businessman" while describing a woman, Minnie Cosby.

SECTION VI

EXERCISES THAT CAN BE LOCALIZED

States and Cities
(Excluding Chapter 12: Writing Obituaries)

CALIFORNIA
Chapter 19 (The News Media and PR Practitioners), Exercise 3, No. 3.

COLORADO

CONNECTICUT
Chapter 7 (Alternative Leads), Exercise 2, Lead 5.

DISTRICT OF COLUMBIA
Chapter 7 (Alternative Leads), Exercise 2, Lead 5.

FLORIDA
Miami: Chapter 19 (News Releases: Working with PR Practitioners), Exercise 6, Vacation Certificates.

GEORGIA
Atlanta: Chapter 6 (Basic News Leads), Exercise 2, Section VI, Lead 2.
Atlanta and Georgia State University: Chapter 17 (Advanced Reporting), Exercise 3.

IOWA
Ames and Iowa State University: Chapter 6 (Basic News Leads), Exercise 2, Section III, Lead 2.

MICHIGAN
East Lansing and Michigan State University: Chapter 7 (Alternative Leads), Exercise 2, Lead 2.

NEBRASKA
Chapter 18 (Writing for Broadcast), Exercise 3, Story 4.

NEVADA
Las Vegas: Chapter 6 (Basic News Leads), Exercise 5, National Beat, Lead 5; Chapter 19 (News Releases: Working with PR Practitioners), Exercise 6, Vacation Certificates.
Reno: Chapter 19 (News Releases: Working with PR Practitioners), Exercise 6, Vacation Certificates.

OHIO
Ohio State University: Chapter 6 (Basic News Leads), Exercise 3, No. 5.

OKLAHOMA

Oklahoma City: Chapter 12 (Speeches and Meetings), Exercise 6.

RHODE ISLAND
Chapter 6 (Basic News Leads), Exercise 5, National Beat, Lead 3.

TENNESSEE
Chapter 9 (Quotations and Attribution), Exercise 3, Story 1.

TEXAS
Dallas: Chapter 8 (The Body of a News Story), Exercise 2, Story 3.
Chapter 19 (The News Media and PR Practitioners), Exercise 3, No. 3

VIRGINIA
Richmond and the University of Richmond: Chapter 17 (Advanced Reporting), Exercise 3.

WISCONSIN
Milwaukee: Chapter 15 (Public Affairs Reporting), Exercise 2.

WYOMING
Chapter 8 (The Body of a News Story), Exercise 3, Story 4.

NATION'S 40 LARGEST CITIES
Chapter 17 (Advanced Reporting), Exercise 4.

ALL 50 STATES
Chapter 17 (Advanced Reporting), Exercise 5.
Chapter 17 (Advanced Reporting), Exercise 6.

SECTION VII

ANSWERS FOR EXERCISES

Chapter 1. The Basics: Format and AP Style

Exercise 1: Format and Copy-Editing Symbol

1. Background Investigations

for $150, three retarde detective s will help you investigate a

potential date roommate, employe or anyone else you are curious

about it

one year ago, the detectives opened Backgrounds Unlimited

and, for $150, will conduct a basic background investigation. The

investigation includes an examination of an individuals

criminal record, driving record, employment history credit

history and educational background

"People have started coming to us, asking us to on check thare their

spouses, tenants nannies -- anyone you nae can imagin," said

Roger datolla, retired who after working 26 years for the city's

police department. His partners, Betsy Aaron and Myron

Hansen, retired after 20 years. "We re friends, and this seemed

like a natural for us," Datolla said. "Were all familiar with

the routine, and its catching on faster than we expected. Of

34

course, some people want us to conduct more detailed investigations, and we charge more for that."

Large corporations ask Backgrounds Unlimited to investigate potential employees. "They want to find out about someone before they hire the person, before it's too late," Datolli continued. "A charming personality isn't enough these days for someone looking for a good job. People in personnel offices realize they can't rely on instinct, references or even diplomas or written employment histories. It's too easy to fake all that. plus, small businesses, especially, don't have the contacts or know-how to conduct good background checks."

Aaron added: "We started off thinking almost all our work would be from businesses, mainly checking on job applicants, possibly employee thefts and that type of thing. Suddenly, we're getting other people, and that part of our business is mushrooming, almost half of what we do now. We've had mothers come in, checking on guys their daughters are dating, and couples checking on neighbors. We even had a college teacher ask us to check on a student he thought was dangerous."

2. Jury Award

A judge Monday ordered the city to pay $2.8 million to Caleb Draia, a thief from Chicago who was shot in the back

35

A police officer fired three shots at Draia, and one hit him, paralyzing him for life.

Draia admitted that he grabbed a purse from 74-year-old Celia Favata as she as was returning to her car in the parking lot at Colonial Mall. He pleaded guilty to a charge of robbery and was sentenced to five years in prison, a term he's now serving.

Draia's lawyer argued that the police were not justified in shooting his client in the back as he fled. A judge agreed, ruling that Draia was the victim of excessive, deadly police force.

Favata testified that she was nearly choked to death. "I tried to holler for help, and he threatened to choke me to death if I didn't shut up," she said. Her glasses were broken, her dress torn, her nose bloodied and her left arm broken when Draia threw her to the ground.

"This wasn't just a mugging," city attorney Allen Farci argued. "This was really a case of attempted murder."

After Judge Marilyn Picott announced her verdict, Favata said: "It's not right. I never got 10 cents, and now this thug gets nearly $3 million. He deserved to be hurt."

Patrolman George Oldaker was shopping at the mall, heard Favata's cries, and saw her lying injured on the ground. "Officer

Oldaker was justified in shooting Draia because he was preventing the flight of a violent felon," the city attorney argued. "There was no other way to stop Draia, to keep him from escaping. No one knew who he was, so if he got away, chances were he'd never be caught."

Farci said he will appeal the judges decision. "Its ludicrous," he said. "This verdict sends a message to people that you can be rewarded if anything happens to you, even if you're hurt while committing a very serious crime. He could've killed that poor old woman.

3. Public Art

Spending money on art is a poor priority and sinful waste of the publics money, Mayor Sabrina datolli said during a press conference friday.

A new state law requires public agencies to spend one-half of 1 percent of the cost of every new government building on art for the building.

"We're planning to build a new city hall, and this law would force us to spend $460,000 on art," Datolli said. "We need that money to erect the city hall, not for art no one in the city wants. Thats a lot of money, all the money we'd typically collect in property taxes in a year from 230 or more homes.

37

That's not what citizens pay their taxes for, not what they want done with their hard-earned money."

Datolli said the state law forces the city to spend on art money also needed for schools, parks, roads and other essential services, including police and fire protection. "Government should limit its spending to essential services, and let private donors and buyers deal in art," Datolli said.

Chairwoman Carmen Foucault, chair of the State Art Federation, said the federation supported the law's passage and will oppose any effort to change it. "We'll do everything we can to fight it," Foucault said. "Government ought to be supporting art and artists. It's important for us as a people, as a culture, to have some public expression of our artistic side, to expose more people to art and culture. Art is an uplifting, civilizing force in our world, and we need more of it. Besides, governments have always subsidized art, and the amount involved here isn't all that significant."

Exercise 2: Format and Copy-Editing Symbols

1. Island Prisons

WASHINGTON, D.C. -- Members of the House Armed Services Committee today recommended that the United States imprison drug addicts and dealers on two remote islands.

THE U.S. Navy plans to abandon its bases on Midway and Wake
Islands, and committee members said the basis should be converted
ertted to prisons prisons to alleviate overcrowding at other
federal facilities

"Labor costs in the region are low, and the inmates could be
required to do a lot more themselas," sad Sen. arlen Hoyniak, D-Ill
Ill "Plus, this would be a real punishmnet and deterrent ."

Midway is 1 mile wide and 15 miles long, and locat 1,150
miles northwest of Hawaii. Wake is a three-square mile atoll
located abotu 2,300 miles wet west of Hawaii. I t was the sitte
of decisive U.S. naval victory during World War II.

Since World War II, the islands have been U.S. possessions, and
the military used has them for emergency airfields and communication
munications stations.

Hoyniak proposed the idea, and the Armed Services Committee
voted unanimously in favo r of it. The committee wants the
secretary of defense to study idea the and report back to it

"Sending drug criminals to faraway islands makes more sense
than building new prisons," Hoyniak said. He axxed added that the
Pacific islands could be reserve for volunters. As an incentive,
he suggeysted that convicts who agreed to be imprisoned on the
islands could have their sentences reduced by one-third

"There's not much change they're going to get anything but rehabilitated on As little islands like these, and the islands are isolated enough to deter any thought of escpe," hoyniak continued. "You can't go anywhere. The only thing prisoners can do there is think about thare mistakes and how they'd improve their lives."

Hoyniak said he thought of the idea after visiting Midway and Wake during committee trips. Neither iland island has any native inhabitants, only military personnel.

However, Nicole Ezzell, director of Humanity International in new York, City considers the idea a giant step backward. "This is astonishing," she said. "It takes penology back two centuries, to the days when the British shipped their hardened criminals off to Australia and the French sent their convicts to Devil's Island off coast the of South america.

2. Truancy

judge JoAnne Kaeppler wednesday sentenced Rosalind McGowan to three days in jail, and McGowans husband Bill, will be giv a three-day sentence the moment she is released. Kaeppler found that the two failed to make their 5-year-old daghter, Claire, attend school. Claire, a sophomore at kennedy High School, was absent 11 out of 20 days last month, and 10 out of 19 days the previous month, according to school records.

"We generally will not prosecute unless the school system has exhausted every possible way to convince parents to get their kids in school," District Attorney Ramon Hernandez said in an interview today. "Generally, this is the last thing we want to do."

Hernandez added, however, that his staff is also pursuing three other truancy cases. "We want people to take this seriously," he explained. "Children are our future. Hopefully, the McGowens and other parents like them will get the message."

State law requires children between the ages of 6 and 16 to attend school. Violations of the law are a second-degree misdemeanor, punishable by sentences of up to 60 days in jail, six months probation and $500 fines.

The McGowens pleaded guilty to violating the law. In addition to sentencing them to jail, Kaeppler placed them on probation for six months and ordered them to perform 100 hours of community service.

They promised Kaeppler that their daughter would return to classes today, but school officials could not immediately confirm that she was present. The McGowens initially told the

41

judge that their daughter did not want to attend school and that there was nothing they could do to make her.

"Try harder," Kaeppler responded.

The school system normally refers five to 10 cases a year to prosecuters, but the McGowens are the first sentenced parents to jail. "Our system hasn't been very aggressive in forcing the issue," Hernandez said. "In this case the parents had repeated warnings, and we decided it was time to begin cracking down on the problem, especially since kids who aren't in school get into all sorts of other trouble."

Superintendent of Schools Hubbard said he was disappointed that the McGowens had to be prosecuted, but that parents must make their children attend school.

3. Police Sting

The police have arrested 114 people who thought they had inherited $14,000.

"Most every criminal is greedy," Police Chief Barry Kopperud said, "and we appealed to their greed."

The police created a fictitious law firm, then spent $1,100 for a fake sign and for printing and postage to send letters to 441 people wanted on warrants issued in the past three years. Each letter was mailed to the person's last known address and said the recipient had inherited $14,000 from a distant relative. The letter set an appointment time for each person to come to the firm and pick up a check.

Fourteen officers posing as lawyers and their assistants were assigned to donated space and worked from there 8 a.m. to 9 p.m. Monday through Friday last week. Recipients who appeared to collect their money were led to a back room and quietly arrested.

Kopertud said officers are often unable to find people wanted on warrants. "When we go to their homes and try to pick these people up, we often miss them, and that warns them we're after them. They disappear, staying with friends or relatives or moving to other cities."

Detective Manuel Cortez added: "This was a good tactic. I don't have any qualms about telling a little white lie to criminals trying to escape the law. Besides, it saved a ton of money. Normally, to make these arrests would take hundreds of hours of our time, and some of these people would commit new crimes before we caught them, if we caught them at all."

Most of the people police arrested were wanted for probation violations, drunken driving, writing bad checks, failure to pay

43

child support and other nonviolent crimes. However, seven were

wanted for burglary, three for car theft, three for robbery and

one for aiding an escape.

Exercise 3: AP Style

1. Next Summer, Maurice Reimer, an accountant with an office

on Bender Ave., wants to buy a 4-door toyota avalon that costs

about $29,000 dollars.

2. Atty. Miguel Acevedo, who lives on Bell Ave., said his

seven-yr.-old son received serious injuries when hit by the

drunken driver in a ford van.

3. United States Senator Connie Mack, R-Fla., a republican from

Florida, said the social security system is bankrupt and, in ten

years, the Federal Government will slash its benefits.

4. Prof. Denise Bealle, a member of the History Dept.,

estimated that one-third of her students will seek a Masters

Degree within 5 years.

5. Fire totally destroyed the Dries Manufacturing Company at

3130 River Rd., and the damage is estimated at $4 million to

$5 million 5,000,000 dollars.

6. The man boy, an 18-year-old College Freshman, arrived in Green

Bay, Wis. at 12 noon and will stay until February 14th.

7. 50 youths met in the YMCA at 3010 1st Avenue yesterday and agreed to return at 7:00PM October 4 to view the film titled Sport.

8. Irregardless of the investigations outcome, the thirty two White youths at Colonial high school want Mr. Tony Guarinno to continue as their Coach.

9. During the 1920s, the Federal Government allocated 820,000 dollars for the project, and Mrs. Mildred Berg, who has a Ph.D. in Sociology, said 8% of the money was wasted.

10. On February 14, 1996, the temperature fell to 0 in Athens, Georgia and on February 15th it fell to 14.

11. Yesterday the United States President promised that the United States Congress would help the flood victims in Miss., Ala., Ga., and La.

12. He wants to Xerox copies of the e-mail he received last Spring and to mail copies to 8 members of the Eastwind Homeowners Assn.

13. The jury reached their verdict at 12 midnight November 4th, finding Kevin Blohm, age 41, not guilty of the 3 charges.

14. Doctor Rachael Rosolowski, of Boston, said the X-rays taken yesterday reveal that the Popes cancer is spreading.

15.   Police said the ford mustang driven by Anne Capiello of
8210 University (Boulevard) was traveling (sixty) mph when it
~~collided with~~ struck a tree at the corner of Wilson and Hampshire
Avenues.

16. The building on Grand (Av.) was ~~totally~~ demolished during
the 1980s, and the state legislature yesterday voted 120-14 to
spend ~~14,300,000 million dollars~~ $14.3 million to rebuild it.

17. Four fifths of the hispanic medical students said they
watched the television program entitled "ER" at 10 ~~A.M.~~ p.m. last
(Thur.) ~~night.~~

18. (24) women, led by (Prof.) Maxine Cessarini, met at 9:00 p.m.
last night and concluded that their children's (3rd) grade teacher
lacks a Bachelor's Degree and lied at the P.T.A. meeting held
last Aug. 29~~th~~.

19. Michael Beverly, ~~age~~ (three), and his baby sitter, Trina
Lasiter found $3,000 ~~dollars~~ on Wilson (Ave.) yesterday, and his
parents have hired (Atty.) Enrique Diaz to represent them.

20. The chemistry major ran south towards the Graumann
Building and, afterwards, explained that she was late for a
meeting with ~~his~~ her adviser and, ~~ir~~regardless of the outcome, will
transfer to another college.

Chapter 2. Grammar and Spelling

Exercise 1. Recognizing and Correcting Newswriting Errors

The textbook provides an answer key for this exercise. See Appendix D. Several of the sentences in this exercise can be corrected in a number of ways. The sentences shown in Appendix are suggested or model answers — not the only possible answers.

Exercise 2. Spelling

1. a lot/~~alot~~
2. acceptable/~~acceeptible~~
3. ~~accidently~~/accidentally
4. accommodate/~~accomodate~~
5. advertising/~~advertizing~~
6. adviser/~~advisor~~
7. afterward/~~afterwards~~
8. ~~alright~~/all right
9. baptize/~~baptise~~
10. ~~boy friend~~/boyfriend
11. broccoli/~~brocolli~~
12. canceled/~~cancelled~~
13. ~~catagorized~~/categorized
14. cemetery/~~cemetary~~
15. ~~comming~~/coming
16. ~~commited~~/committed
17. ~~congradulations~~/ congratulations
18. conscious/~~concious~~
19. ~~contraversial~~/controversial
20. ~~credability~~/credibility
21. ~~critized~~/criticized
22. ~~cryed~~/cried
23. defendant/~~defendent~~
24. ~~desert~~/dessert (food)
25. despite/~~dispite~~
26. ~~deterrant~~/deterrent
27. ~~dilema~~/dilemma
28. disastrous/~~disasterous~~
29. ~~dispise~~/despise
30. elite/~~elete~~
31. ~~embarass~~/embarrass
32. emphasize/~~emphacize~~
33. ~~employe~~/employee
34. endorsed/~~indorsed~~
35. ~~exhorbitant~~/exorbitant
36. ~~existance~~/existence
37. ~~explaination~~/explanation
38. fascination/~~facination~~
39. ~~favortism~~/favoritism
40. ~~Febuary~~/February
41. ~~fourty~~/forty
42. ~~fulfil~~/fulfill
43. glamour/~~glamor~~
44. ~~goverment~~/government
45. guerrilla/~~guerilla~~
46. harassment/~~harrassment~~
47. humorous/~~humerous~~
48. ~~independant~~/independent
49. indispensable/~~indispensible~~
50. ~~infered~~/inferred
51. innuendo/~~inuendo~~
52. ~~irrate~~/irate
53. ~~irregardless~~/regardless
54. ~~it's~~/its (possessive)
55. ~~janiter~~/janitor
56. ~~judgement~~/judgment
57. kindergarten/~~kindergarden~~
58. license/~~liscense~~
59. lightning/~~lightening~~
60. ~~likelyhood~~/likelihood
61. magazines/~~magasines~~
62. municipal/~~municiple~~
63. ~~nickles~~/nickels
64. noticeable/~~noticable~~
65. occasionally/~~ocassionally~~
66. ~~occured~~/occurred
67. ~~oppertunity~~/opportunity
68. ~~per-cent~~/percent
69. ~~permissable~~/permissible
70. ~~personel~~/personnel
71. ~~persue~~/pursue
72. ~~picknicking~~/picnicking
73. plagiarism/~~plagarism~~
74. practice/~~practise~~
75. ~~priviledge~~/privilege
76. protester/~~protestor~~
77. questionnaire/~~questionaire~~
78. receive/~~recieve~~
79. reckless/~~wreckless~~
80. re-elect/~~reelect~~
81. ~~refering~~/referring
82. ~~reguardless~~/regardless
83. ~~resturant~~/restaurant
84. ~~roomate~~/roommate
85. ~~saleries~~/salaries
86. sandwich/~~sandwhich~~
87. ~~seige~~/siege
88. separate/~~seperate~~
89. sergeant/~~sargeant~~
90. sizable/~~sizeable~~
91. ~~sophmore~~/sophomore
92. souvenir/~~sovenir~~
93. stab/~~stabb~~
94. ~~strickly~~/strictly
95. suing/~~sueing~~
96. summarize/~~summerize~~
97. surgery/~~surgury~~
98. surprise/~~surprize~~
99. taxi/~~taxy~~
100. teen-ager/~~teenager~~
101. temperature/~~temperture~~
102. ~~tendancy~~/tendency
103. their/~~thier~~
104. totaled/~~totalled~~
105. toward/~~towards~~
106. ~~transfered~~/transferred
107. tries/~~trys~~
108. ~~truely~~/truly
109. until/~~untill~~
110. ~~useable~~/usable
111. ~~vacinate~~/vaccinate
112. vacuum/~~vaccum~~
113. valedictorian/~~valdictorian~~
114. vetoes/~~vetos~~
115. ~~victum~~/victim
116. villain/~~villan~~

117. Wednesday/~~Wedesday~~
118. ~~wierd~~/weird
119. writing/~~writting~~
120. yield/~~yeild~~

Exercise 3. Spelling

1. ~~abberation~~/aberration
2. abbreviate/~~abreviate~~
3. abdomen/~~abdoman~~
4. absence/~~absense~~
5. accessible/~~accessable~~
6. ~~acknowlegement~~/acknowledgment
7. acquaintance/~~acquantance~~
8. ~~acter~~/actor
9. ~~adherant~~/adherent
10. ~~admissable~~/admissible
11. ~~admited~~/admitted
12. affidavit/~~afidavit~~
13. ~~allready~~/already
14. ~~alotted~~/~~alloted~~/allotted
15. alphabet/~~alphebet~~
16. ambulance/~~ambulence~~
17. ~~ammendment~~/amendment
18. among/~~amoung~~
19. apologize/~~apologise~~
20. ~~apparantly~~/apparently
21. ~~arguement~~/argument
22. ~~arithematic~~/arithmetic
23. assassinate/~~assasinate~~
24. athlete/~~athlite~~
25. auxiliary/~~auxillary~~
26. ax/~~axe~~
27. baby-sit/~~baby-sit~~
28. bachelor's/~~bachelors~~ degree
29. backward/~~backwards~~
30. baloney/~~balogna~~
31. barbecue/~~barbeque~~
32. basically/~~basicly~~
33. becoming/~~becomming~~
34. ~~believeable~~/~~beleivable~~/believable
35. beneficial/~~benificial~~
36. broadcast/~~broadcasted~~
37. ~~bureacracy~~/bureaucracy
38. burglars/~~burglers~~
39. Caribbean/~~Carribean~~
40. ~~catagorized~~/categorized
41. catalog/catalogue
42. catastrophe/~~catastraphe~~
43. champagne/~~champayne~~
44. changeable/~~changable~~
45. chauffeur/~~chaufeur~~
46. cigarettes/~~cigaretes~~
47. ~~commited~~/committed
48. comparable/~~comperable~~
49. ~~concensus~~/consensus
50. contemptible/~~contemptable~~
51. ~~definately~~/definitely
52. demagogue/~~demogog~~
53. dependent/~~dependant~~
54. ~~desireable~~/desirable
55. destroyed/~~distroyed~~
56. ~~deterant~~/~~deterrant~~/deterrent
57. develop/~~develope~~
58. ~~deviding~~/dividing
59. ~~disasterous~~/disastrous
60. discrimination/~~descrimination~~
61. drunkenness/~~drunkeness~~
62. exaggerate/~~exagerate~~
63. existence/~~existance~~
64. expelled/~~expeled~~
65. familiar/~~familar~~
66. fiery/~~fierey~~
67. forward/~~forwards~~
68. ~~fourty~~/forty
69. ~~goodby~~/goodbye
70. grammar/~~grammer~~
71. ~~guarante~~/guarantee
72. ~~hazzard~~/hazard
73. hemorrhage/~~hemorrage~~
74. ~~heros~~/heroes
75. ~~hitchiker~~/hitchhiker
76. imminent/~~imminant~~
77. ~~imposter~~/impostor
78. innuendo/~~inuendo~~
79. ~~involveing~~/involving
80. ~~labelled~~/labeled
81. ~~layed~~/laid
82. liaison/liason
83. ~~likeable~~/likable
84. limousine/~~limousene~~
85. loneliness/~~lonelyness~~
86. ~~maintnance~~/maintenance
87. mathematics/~~mathmatics~~
88. ~~medias~~/media (plural)
89. millionaire/~~millionnaire~~
90. missile/~~missle~~
91. misspell/~~mispell~~
92. mortgage/~~morgage~~
93. ~~mosquitos~~/mosquitoes
94. ~~necesary~~/necessary
95. omitted/~~ommited~~
96. ~~paniced~~/panicked
97. ~~payed~~/paid
98. persistent/~~persistant~~
99. perspiration/~~persperation~~
100. potatoes/~~potatos~~
101. ~~practise~~/practice
102. precede/~~preceed~~
103. preparing/~~prepairing~~
104. prevalent/~~prevalant~~
105. professor/~~proffessor~~
106. prominent/~~prominant~~
107. ~~pryed~~/pried
108. ~~realised~~/realized
109. receive/~~recieve~~
110. repetition/~~repitition~~
111. ~~resturant~~/restaurant
112. saboteur/~~sabateur~~
113. sheriff/~~sherrif~~
114. singular/~~singuler~~
115. ~~sophmore~~/sophomore
116. survivors/~~survivers~~
117. ~~tenative~~/tentative
118. traveled/~~travelled~~
119. wintry/~~wintery~~
120. ~~worrys~~/worries

Chapter 3. Newswriting Style

Exercise 2. Being Concise

SECTION I: USING SIMPLE WORDS
1. **Accelerate:** quicken, speed up, hasten, hurry.
2. **Endeavor:** as a noun—attempt, try, effort, struggle, purpose. As a verb—attempt, aim, strive, work.
3. **Ultimate:** final, latest, last, utmost.
4. **Depart:** leave, go, withdraw.
5. **Imbibe:** drink, guzzle, gulp.
6. **Reside:** live, dwell, occupy, remain, stay.
7. **Massive:** big, huge, large, immense.
8. **Utilize:** use, employ.
9. **Incarcerate:** jail, confine, detain.
10. **Apprehend:** arrest, seize, capture, catch.
11. **Deceased:** dead, late.
12. **Minimize:** lessen, reduce, diminish, dwindle.
13. **Lacerations:** cuts, gashes, slashes.
14. **Currently:** now.
15. **Locate:** find, discover, determine, unearth.
16. **Inquire:** ask, question, probe, grill.
17. **Feasible:** possible, attainable, workable.
18. **Stated:** said, told, revealed.
19. **Obtained:** got, took, recovered, grabbed, gained.
20. **Commence:** begin, start, cause, make, do, trigger, spark, occur.

SECTION II: AVOIDING REDUNDANT PHRASES
1. complete
2. rejected
3. expert
4. costs
5. small
6. gunman
7. truth
8. plans
9. predicament
10. engulfed
11. body
12. calm
13. genius
14. destroyed
15. blame
16. postponed
17. free
18. filled
19. crisis
20. my opinion

SECTION III: AVOIDING WORDY PHRASES
1. much; plenty
2. because
3. near
4. hopes
5. consider
6. married
7. then
8. left
9. consensus
10. despite
11. approved
12. decided
13. motioned
14. said
15. now
16. had; possessed
17. injured
18. know
19. end; finish
20. if

SECTION IV: ELIMINATING UNNECESSARY WORDS
1. Anyone may participate.
2. The robbers also took some liquor.
3. The company employs about 50 truck drivers.

4.   The nationwide poll showed that 41 percent support the bill.

5.   Police officers began the investigation.

SECTION V: REWRITING WORDY SENTENCES

1.   He said the program will cost about $500.

2.   The police officer fired six times at the suspect.

3.   Sanchez is in fair condition at Memorial Hospital.

4.   They told the mayor she would have to make an announcement on the decision.

5.   Eight of the 10 stock car drivers said injuries and deaths are possible in their races.

SECTION VI: SIMPLIFYING OVERLOADED SENTENCES

1.   Democratic Sen. Karen Baliet Tuesday introduced a bill banning the sale of disposable diapers, which she said are filling up the state's landfills. **NOTE:** Karen Baliet is listed in the city directory as an advertising executive with Baliet & Associates. She also is a newly elected member of the state Senate.

2.   Police arrested a lone gunman who robbed the Merchants Bank on Main Street Friday after he unknowingly scooped up a device containing red dye and tear gas that exploded when he fled the bank.
       SEXISM ISSUE: Note the use of the word "gunman."

3.   Sales of Apple Computer's newest model exceeded expectations, causing a $1.1 billion backlog of orders, which has angered consumers and investors.

4.   A man threatened the occupants of a vehicle he was following early Wednesday morning, pointing a pistol at them and shouting obscenities.

Exercise 3. -Isms

SECTION I: AVOIDING SEXIST TITLES AND TERMS

1. business person
2. member of Congress; representative
3. crafts worker; artist; artisan
4. councilperson; council member
5. salesperson; sales representative
6. chair; chairperson
7. paper carrier
8. crew; staff; personnel
9. humankind; humanity; people
10. leader; diplomat; politician
11. repairer; technician
12. manufactured; synthetic; artificial

SECTION II: AVOIDING EXCLUSIVELY MALE NOUNS AND PRONOUNS

1.   Reporters are expected to protect their sources.

2.   Good athletes often jog to build their endurance.

3.   Normally, auto mechanics buy their own tools.

4.   No one knows which member of Congress leaked the details.

5.   If patients are clearly dying of cancer, doctors may give them enough drugs to ease their pain, and perhaps even enough to hasten their deaths.

SECTION III: AVOIDING STEREOTYPES

1.   Richard Diaz, a nurse, and Diane Diaz, an author, arrived today.

2.   Police are looking for a man who was seen running from the building after the alarm went off.

3.   Members of the American Indian Movement protested today when federal agents attempted to interrupt a meeting of tribal elders.

4.   A representative for the company announced that it has reached an agreement with the hunters and fishers on their use of the woods.

5.   Paula Valesquez was elected to the university's board of trustees.
6.   City officials announced today that 14 members of the clergy will serve on the committee.

Exercise 4. Testing All Your Skills

SECTION I: AVOIDING REDUNDANT PHRASES
1. buried ~~underground~~
2. ~~first~~ began
3. fume ~~with anger~~
4. closed ~~down~~
5. is ~~now~~
6. combine ~~together~~
7. ~~new~~ innovation
8. found ~~out~~
9. sent ~~away~~ for
10. opened ~~its doors~~
11. responded ~~by saying~~
12. ~~end~~ result
13. ~~positively~~ identified
14. said ~~in the past~~
15. whether ~~or not~~
16. ~~unpaid~~ debt
17. started ~~out~~
18. ~~perfect~~ stranger
19. set a ~~new~~ record
20. ~~now~~ want

SECTION II: ELIMINATING UNNECESSARY WORDS
1.   Health inspectors are ~~in the process of currently~~ investigating the restaurant and may ~~completely~~ close it ~~down~~ in about three to five days.
2.   She spent every summer ~~during her life~~ in the cottage ~~located~~ at Lake Tahoe with her ~~young~~ infant, who is now an attorney ~~at law~~.
3.   It's a ~~very unique~~ problem and, in an effort to prevent another ~~violent~~ explosion, they want to clean up the site at ~~the hour of~~ 2 p.m. regardless of whether ~~or not~~ it's privately owned.
4.   ~~It should be pointed out that~~ after he died last Easter ~~Sunday~~, an autopsy ~~conducted to determine the actual cause of death~~ found that he was, in fact, strangled ~~to death~~.
5.   ~~In the past,~~ he personally assembled ~~together~~ a dozen ~~knowledgeable~~ experts and insisted that they would like the ~~end~~ result regardless of whether ~~or not~~ they were paid.

SECTION III: AVOIDING WORDY PHRASES
1.   The runaway truck struck three cars and a delivery van before it stopped.
2.   Soon, the city council plans to submit a new budget to the mayor.
3.   Police are searching for the ~~lone~~ gunman near Fifth and Main streets.
4.   Prosecutors charged that the witness possessed important evidence.
5.   Local high school athletic games were postponed because of the storm.

SECTION IV: SIMPLIFYING SENTENCES
1.   Gladys Ann Higginbotham said other people also believe the children are in danger.
2.   Thomas Haskell said he is not concerned about the airline's safety because it has a good record.
3.   The driver sped north through the parking lot at an estimated 60 mph.
4.   The girl was taken to Mercy Hospital, where she is listed in critical condition.
5.   It is possible the program could begin to serve about 20 schools in the vicinity when plans are finalized.

SECTION V: AVOIDING SEXUAL STEREOTYPES
1.   A California couple attended the reunion.
2.   While the women were playing tennis, the men were playing golf.
3.   Valerie Dawkins is a stay-at-home mother who participates in politics.
4.   Celia J. Favata, 56, won the city's Senior Women's Tennis Tournament.

5.   Council member Alice Cycler is fighting to improve the city's parks.

SECTION VI: REMAINING OBJECTIVE
1.   ~~Lucky to be alive today,~~ the 20-year-old man walked away uninjured from a car accident ~~that could have been fatal.~~
2.   ~~What began as a routine day ended tragically for~~ Albert Wei ~~when he~~ was shot in the face during a ~~daring~~ daylight robbery.
3.   The mayor's speech was ~~well-received, as he was~~ interrupted more than 20 times by ~~hearty~~ applause.
4.   When they got home, the young couple ~~had a big surprise. They~~ found that burglars had taken all their ~~lovely~~ wedding presents, leaving only the wrapping paper and ribbon behind.
5.   Forty-five people ~~miraculously~~ escaped injury when the bus they were riding in overturned on a ~~perilous~~ stretch of interstate highway near Philadelphia.

VII: TESTING ALL YOUR SKILLS
1.   He said the disturbance hurt the school's image
2.   The group's fight against plans to improve the road will have to wait until an engineering study can be completed.
3.   A resident from the eighth floor opposed the condominium board's proposal.
4.   A journalism professor's class found that over three years 19 women at the university were sexually assualted.
5.   Eight people served on the committee.

Exercise 5. Review

The textbook provides an answer key for students who complete this exercise. See Appendix D.

Chapter 4. The Language of News

Exercise 1. Vocabulary

1. **About** means having to do with, concerning or in connection with. **Around** means close to or near.

2. **Above** means overhead. **Over** refers to spatial relationships: The plane flew over the city. Use **more than** with numbers: He has more than $100.

3. **Adapt** means to change or adjust something to make it fit or suitable: It took a year for them to adapt to city life. **Adept** means to be highly skilled or expert at something: She was adept at playing the violin. **Adopt** means to choose, such as adopting a child, or to take an idea and use it as your own or to vote to accept something such as an amendment, ordinance or motion.

4. **Advice** is a noun meaning an opinion given as to what to do; counsel. **Advise** is the verb form meaning to give advice to or to counsel.

5. **Affect** means to act on or to produce an effect or change. **Effect** is the consequence or result.

6. **Aid** means to give help or assistance. An **aide** is someone who helps or assists.

7. An **alley** is a narrow street or walk usually behind a row of buildings. An **ally**, as a noun, is an individual, organization or country joined with another for a common purpose. As a verb, **ally** means to unite for a specific purpose.

8. **Allude** means to refer in a casual or indirect way. **Elude** means to avoid, escape or evade.

9. An **altar** is a table or stand used for sacred purposes in a place of worship. **Alter** means to make different or modify something.

10. Use **alumnus** when referring to a man who has attended a school. **Alumni** is the plural form of alumnus. Use **alumna** when referring to a woman who has attended a school. **Alumnae** is the plural form of alumna. Use **alumni** when referring to a group of men and women.

11. **Between** introduces two items and **among** introduces more than two. However, AP style notes that **between** is the correct word when expressing the relationships of three or more items that are considered one pair at a time.

12. An **anecdote** is a short, entertaining personal or biographical story. An **antidote** is a remedy to counteract a poison or some unwanted condition.

13. An **angel** is a supernatural being of more than human power and intelligence, or a guiding spirit. An **angle** is a sharp corner; a point of view; to use tricks to get something; or to fish with a hook and line.

14. Statisticians employ several measures of central tendency or ways to describe the central value around which a group of scores clusters. The most common indicator of central tendency is the **average** or **mean**. The mean is found by adding a group of scores and then dividing by the number of scores in the group. Another measure of central tendency is the **median**. This is the value above and below which half the scores lie. A third measure of central tendency is the **mode**, or most frequent score. This is simply the score obtained by more people in the group than any other score.

15. A **bazaar** is a shop for selling a variety of goods or a sale of various items for fund-raising purposes. **Bizarre** means something odd in manner or appearance, or unexpected or unbelievable.

16. **Because** means reason or cause. **Since** is related to time: They arrived last week and have been here ever since.

17. **Bloc** means an alliance or group that acts as a single unit, as a coalition of voters; a political bloc. **Block** has many meanings; however, they do not include a political alliance.

18. **Blond** is used as a noun for men and as an adjective: He and she have blond hair. Use **blonde** as

a noun for females: The blonde wore a blue dress.

19. **Born** means to be brought into life or being. It also means having certain qualities innately: A born athlete. **Borne** is a past participle of bear meaning to give birth to.

20. A **burglar** is someone who illegally enters a building with the intent to steal money or property. A **robber** threatens or actually uses force or violence to steal. A **swindler** uses fraud or deceit to cheat people out of money or property. A thief is anyone who steals without force, often secretly.

21. A **calendar** is a system for arranging time into days, weeks, months and years; or a list or schedule of something, such as pending court cases. A **calender** is a machine with rollers between which paper or cloth is run to give it a smooth or glossy finish.

22. **Canvas** is a course cloth used for tents, sails or oil paintings. **Canvass** means to examine or discuss something in detail; or to ask for votes, opinions or orders.

23. A **capital** is a city that serves as a seat of government, especially for a state or country; also, **capital** may be used in reference to money. A **capitol** is a building that houses the legislative branch of government.

24. To **censor** means to suppress parts of a work such as a book, article, play or movie considered objectionable. To **censure** means to disapprove, criticize, blame or condemn; a censure is an official reprimand.

25. **Choose** means to pick out or select something. **Chose** is the past tense of choose.

26. To **cite** means to quote or use as an example. **Sight** involves vision; the act of seeing. A **site** is a location.

27. To **complement** means to complete, fit in with, make perfect or make whole. To **compliment** is to flatter or praise.

28. To **compose** means to create, form or put together. It is used in both the active and passive voices. To **comprise** means to include or contain or be made up of certain things. It is used in the active voice and followed by a direct object. **Constitute** means to establish a law, government or institution; to set up something in a legal form, such as an assembly or proceeding.

29. A **confidant** is a close personal friend to whom one tells secrets. Someone who is **confident** is assured or certain about something.

30. **Conscience** means a knowledge or sense of right and wrong with a compulsion to do right. **Conscious** is having a feeling or knowledge; aware; cognizant.

31. A **council** is a deliberative body and the people who are members of it. To **counsel** means to advise. A **consul** is a government official appointed to live in a foreign city and serve his country's citizens and business interests there.

32. You may be **convinced** of something by argument or proof. You must be **persuaded** to do something.

33. A **criterion** is a standard rule or test by which something can be judged. **Criteria** is the plural of criterion.

34. As a noun, **damage** means injury or harm resulting in a loss. As a verb, **damage** means to injure or harm something. **Damages** generally is used as a legal term meaning money to be paid to compensate for injury or loss.

35. A **datum** is a fact or figure from which conclusions can be inferred; information. **Data** is the plural form of datum.

36. **Decent** means that something or someone conforms to approved social standards; respectable. **Descent** means coming or going down. **Dissent** means to disagree.

37. As a noun, a **desert** is a dry, barren, sandy wilderness. As a transitive verb, **desert** means to abandon one's post or duties without permission. **Dessert** is a course at the end of a meal consisting of pie, cake or ice cream.

38. **Discreet** means being careful about what one says; being prudent. **Discrete** means unrelated;

separate and distinct.

39. **Elusive** means slippery, fleeting or difficult to grasp. **Illusive** means deceptive or misleading.

40. One who leaves a country **emigrates** from it. One who comes into a country **immigrates**.

41. **Ensure** means to guarantee: They wanted to ensure that the work would be done properly. **Insure** refers to a contract guaranteeing monetary reimbursement after a loss of life or property: The policy will insure her life.

42. **Entitled** means having a right to do, give or have something. **Titled** means having a name. For example, a book, poem or play is titled.

43. **Envelop** means to surround or cover completely. An **envelope** is a folded paper container for letters or the bag that contains the gas in a dirigible or balloon.

44. **Fair** means just and honest or impartial; beautiful and unblemished. A **fair** also can refer to a festival or carnival. **Fare** refers to the cost of a trip in a train, plane or taxi. **Fare** also can refer to a specific condition: She fared well in school.

45. **Farther** refers to physical distance: She walked farther than anyone. **Further** refers to an extension of time or degree: Police will investigate further into the murder.

46. Use **fewer** when writing about a number of individual items. Use **less** when referring to bulk, amount, sum, time or concept: The school has fewer than 1,000 students. She has less money than the other students.

47. A **fiance** is a man engaged to be married. A **fiancee** is a woman engaged to be married.

48. A **foreword** is an introductory statement or remark at the beginning of a speech or book. **Forward** pertains to motion; advancing toward. Someone who is **forward** is bold or presumptuous.

49. **Fourth** refers to a quarter of something or to the fourth in a series. **Forth** means forward, away from a place, or onward in time, order or a series.

50. **Foul** means someone or something is stinking or loathsome; wicked or obscene; stormy or unfavorable. **Foul** also means not according to the rules. **Fowl** refers to any species of bird.

51. One **hangs** a picture, a criminal or oneself. **Hanged** is used for past tense or the passive voice when referring to executions or suicides. **Hung** is used to describe the hanging of objects, such as pictures.

52. To **imply** means to suggest, signify or mean. To **infer** means to draw a conclusion from something that has been said.

53. To **incite** means to stimulate or promote; to arouse a mob. **Insight** means understanding, especially through intuition.

54. **It's** is the contraction for "it is." **Its** is the possessive form of belonging to or done by it.

55. Generally, **lay** means to put or place, and it requires a direct object. **Lie** means to recline and does not take a direct object.

56. **Liable** means to be legally bound or responsible. **Libel** is any false and malicious statement, picture or other printed material that unjustly damages a person's reputation. **Likely** is an adjective meaning credible or probable; or suitable or promising.

57. **Loose** means free, not confined or restrained. **Lose** means to be unable to find, keep or maintain.

58. A **marshal** is a military or court officer or a law enforcement officer with duties similar to those of a sheriff. **Marshall** is the name of some people and a group of islands in the Pacific Ocean.

59. A **medium** is a means of communication that reaches the general public. **Media** is the plural form of medium.

60. A **miner** is a person whose work is digging coal or other minerals in a mine. A **minor** is someone who is under full legal age. As an adjective, **minor** can mean lesser in size or importance.

61. **Moral** is the opposite of immoral; it involves an ethical judgment or principle; right conduct or behavior. **Morale** refers to a mental condition, such as an individual or group's cheerfulness, confidence or enthusiasm.

62. **Naval** pertains to a navy and its ships and personnel. A **navel** is a bellybutton.

63. An **ordinance** is a governmental statute or regulation. **Ordnance** pertains to military weapons and hardware.

64. A **pedal** is a lever operated by foot. **Peddle** means to go from place to place selling small items.

65. Use **person** when referring to an individual. Use **people** when referring to more than one individual. Use **persons** only in a direct quote or as part of an organization's title.

66. **Personal** means private or individual, or involving human beings. **Personnel** are people employed in an organization.

67. A **phenomenon** is any fact or experience that is unusual or can be explained by science. **Phenomena** is the plural form of phenomenon.

68. A **plague** is a deadly epidemic disease or anything that afflicts or troubles. A **plaque** is a wall tablet commemorating or identifying something.

69. A **pole** is a long slender piece of wood or metal used for support or for propelling a boat or raft. A **poll** is the canvassing of a selected or random group of people to collect information. A **poll** also is a place where people vote in an election.

70. As a noun, a **pore** is a small opening in the skin or in leaves. As an intransitive verb, **pore** means to read or study carefully. **Pour** means to make flow in a continuous stream, to flow freely and copiously.

71. **Pray** means to implore a higher or supreme being to intercede on one's behalf. **Prey** means to plunder, rob or profit by swindling: The gang members preyed on the school children. As a noun, **prey** is the person or thing that falls victim to someone or something: The hunters saw their prey coming out of the woods.

72. A **principal** is something of the highest rank, often a chief or the head of a school. Or, it may refer to a sum of money. A **principle** is an accepted rule of conduct, a basic law or an assumption.

73. To **ravage** means to devastate or destroy through the use of violence. **Ravish** means to abduct, rape or carry away. Soldiers can ravish a woman, but not a building.

74. **Receive** means to take, get or bear something. **Suffer** means to undergo something painful or unpleasant; to endure. **Sustain** means to maintain or prolong, to confirm or support.

75. A **reign** is the period during which a particular king or queen rules a country. A **rein** is a strap or harness used to control an animal.

76. A **role** is a part in a play or a customary function, such as the role of a teacher. To **roll** means to move something along a surface so that it revolves, or to move it on wheels. A **roll** may also be a list of names.

77. A **statue** is artwork of realistic or abstract form made of metal, stone, wood or clay. A **statute** is a law passed by a legislative body.

78. **Than** is used for comparisons. **Then** is used to refer to a particular time.

79. Use **that** and **which** in referring to inanimate objects and animals without names. **That** is used in restrictive clauses and is not set off with commas. **Which** is used in nonrestrictive clauses and is set off with commas.

80. There is a possessive pronoun: They ordered their dinner. **There** is an adverb indicating direction: They went there for dinner. **There** also is used as an impersonal pronoun: There was no silverware on the table. **They're** is a contraction for "they are."

81. **To** refers to direction, belonging or comparison. **Too** means in addition or more than enough.

82. A **trail** is a path. As a transitive verb, **trail** means to hunt by tracking. A **trial** is a formal legal proceeding testing validity of charges brought against an individual or organization. **Trial** also can mean suffering or hardship; a test.

83. A **trustee** helps administer an organization. A **trusty** is a prison inmate considered reliable enough to have special duties and privileges.

84. **Waive** means to give up or forgo a right or claim; to postpone. **Wave** means to move up and down or back and forth in a curving motion; to signal by moving the hand to and fro; to brandish.

85. **Weather** is the general condition of the atmosphere. **Whether** means in case or in either case.

86. **Who** and **whom** are used for references to human beings and to animals with a name. **Who** is used when someone is the subject of a sentence, clause or phrase: The man who fired the shots was arrested. Who is there? **Whom** is used when someone is the object of a verb or preposition: The man to whom the gun was sold fired the shots. Whom did you call?

87. **Who's** is the contraction of "who is" or "who was." **Whose** indicates possession.

88. **Your** is a possessive pronoun. **You're** is a contraction for "you are."

Exercise 2. Vocabulary

1. The federal (marshal/~~marshall~~) said (~~its~~/it's) a peculiar (~~cite~~/~~sight~~/site) for the building and may (affect/~~effect~~) employees' (~~moral~~/morale).

2. He said it will cost (about/~~around~~) $5,000 to send a dozen (people/~~persons~~) to the state capital/~~Capitol~~) to speak to the governor's (~~aids~~/aides).

3. The (blond/~~blonde~~) said he (~~complemented~~/complimented) the reporter's skill but felt (their/~~there~~/~~they're~~) three (media/~~medium~~) hurt the (principal's/~~principles~~) reputation.

4. The U.S. Army general was able to (envelop/~~envelope~~) the enemy in (fewer/~~less~~) than 24 hours, capturing (more than/~~over~~) 7,000 soldiers (who/~~whom~~/~~which~~) were (~~than~~/then) disarmed.

5. Rather (than/~~then~~) (~~censor~~/censure) the nine bank (trustees/~~trusties~~) behavior, he wants a new state (ordinance/~~ordnance~~) to govern (their/~~there~~/~~they're~~) behavior.

6. He (~~adviced~~/advised) the investors to (~~altar~~/alter) their plans (because/~~since~~) it would be difficult to (ensure/~~insure~~) everyone's cooperation.

7. Despite the bad (weather/~~whether~~), the mayor's (~~aid~~/aide) said a large (bloc/~~block~~) of voters appeared at the hearing and opposed buying the (desert/~~dessert~~) (~~cite~~/~~sight~~/site) for a park.

8. Her (fiance/~~fiancee~~), a (blond/~~blonde~~) (~~alumna~~/~~alumnae~~/~~alumni~~/alumnus) of Harvard, wants to (~~lay~~/lie) down.

9. (More than/~~over~~) a dozen (~~persons~~/people) (~~received~~/suffered/~~sustained~~) injuries during the storm that occurred (~~about~~/around) 8 p.m., and the minister was (praying/~~preying~~) for (their/~~there~~/~~they're~~) recovery.

10. After looking at a (calendar/~~calender~~) they decided to (~~canvas~~/canvass) the city's voters and are (~~confidant~~/confident) that most want the woman's (~~statute~~/statue) erected in the park.

11. The children said (their/~~there~~/~~they're~~) families (~~emigrated~~/immigrated) from Asia and are (~~liable~~/~~libel~~/likely) to move (farther/~~further~~) South.

12. They were (~~adapt~~/adept/~~adopt~~) at (~~convincing~~/persuading) the officials to reread the stacks of (data/~~datum~~) and (~~altar~~/alter) the seven (criteria/~~criterion~~) for (choosing/~~chosing~~) an architect.

13. The book (~~entitled~~/titled) "Betrayal" estimates that the (~~trail~~/trial) will last (fewer/~~less~~) than 10 days, and (implies/~~infers~~) that the jury will find the defendant (innocent/~~not guilty~~).

14. They (~~hanged~~/hung) the controversial painting in a school hallway and want to know (~~who's~~/whose) side (~~your~~/you're) likely to favor.

15. Her (~~aid~~/aide) fell (~~foreword~~/forward) but remained (~~conscience~~/conscious), (~~receiving~~/suffering/~~sustaining~~) only (~~miner~~/minor) cuts and bruises.

16. The path's steep (~~decent~~/descent/~~dissent~~) made it difficult for bicyclists to (pedal/~~peddle~~) (farther/~~further~~) south.

17. The jury, (that/which) was (composed/comprised) of seven men and five women, convicted the defendant of (liable/libel) and, after the (trail/trial), jurors explained that they did not care (weather/whether) she was apologetic.
18. The carriage began to (role/roll) (foreword/forward) and a (loose/lose) wheel broke off, making it impossible to travel any (farther/further).
19. To improve the scouts' (moral/morale), they (choose/chose) a 60-foot metal flag (pole/poll) and placed a (plague/plaque) on (its/it's) concrete base.
20. The (forth/fourth) group of veterans entered the (alley/ally), which veers South at a 45-degree (angel/angle), (then/than) marched seven more (blocs/blocks).

Exercise 3. Vocabulary

1. The woman, an (emigrant/immigrant) (born/borne) in Ireland's (capital/Capitol) of Dublin, said she wants to (aid/aide) the nine-member city (consul/council/counsel).
2. To (ensure/insure) (its/it's) success, editors (altared/altered) the (medias/medium's) content, increasing its circulation and prestige.
3. Following (their/there/they're) minister's (advice/advise), (more than/over) 100 (people/persons) (who/which) volunteered to help address the (envelops/envelopes) appeared at 7 p.m.
4. The (statue/statute) of a misshapen (angel/angle) on the church (altar/alter) caused a (miner/minor) controversy.
5. The book, (entitled/titled) "Western Justice," reported that seven rustlers (who's/whose) names are unknown were (hanged/hung) (about/around) seven miles from the (desert/dessert) (cite/sight/site).
6. As a matter of (principal/principle), the prison (trustee/trusty) tried to (affect/effect) the five (criteria/criterion) (cited/sighted/sited) by the warden, (who/whom/which) dislikes the proposal's cost.
7. People (who/which) use the bicycle (trail/trial) said (its/it's) (to/too) dangerous: that several (received/suffered/sustained) serious injuries as they tried to (pedal/peddle) (farther/further) north.
8. The club's (trustees/trusties) were (adapt/adept/adopt) at (convincing/persuading) the base's (naval/navel) (personal/personnel) to (waive/wave) their right to use the facilities.
9. While preparing the (calendar/calender), the school's (principal/principle) warned that (fewer/less) than a dozen parents were likely (to/too) (aid/aide) the teachers (who/whom/that) will need (more than/over) 100 volunteers.
10. They wonder (weather/whether) (your/you're) likely to (lose/loose) the major (role/roll) in the play or are (confidant/confident) of success.
11. Her (fiance/fiancee) (implied/inferred) that the team's (moral/morale) fell (because/since) the coach was replaced after allegedly (praying/preying) upon vulnerable young males.
12. An (alumna/alumnae/alumni/alumnus) of the university started her speech with an (anecdote/antidote), then said all the (data/datum) revealed that the company's (personal/personnel) knew about the danger.
13. He called the incident (bazaar/bizarre) and explained that the (burglar/robber/swindler/thief) who broke into his home (ravaged/ravished) only a closet.
14. Rather (than/then) immediately (choose/chose) a new stereo, the (blond/blonde) decided to (convince/persuade) her parents to give her (about/around) $200 more, (citing/sighting/siting) its high cost.
15. (Censors/censures) objected to the nude children drawn on the large (canvas/canvass) (hanged/hung) in a faculty members office, insisting that it was not (decent/descent/dissent).
16. The speaker (implied/inferred) that the city (ordinance/ordnance) will require the bus company to raise its (fairs/fares) by (more than/over) 50 percent.

17. He (~~complemented~~/complimented) all the teams but said the girls in the (~~forth~~/fourth) lane swam (farther/~~further~~) than any of their competitors.

18. She remained (~~conscience~~/conscious) but said the (foul/~~fowl~~) odor was (~~liable~~/~~libel~~/likely) to make other (people/~~persons~~) sick regardless of (~~weather~~/whether) they entered the room.

19. The brothers found the broken (pole/~~poll~~) in an (alley/~~ally~~) about a (~~bloc~~/block) from (their/~~there~~/~~they're~~) home and said (more than/~~over~~) 100 (people/~~persons~~) had been in the area.

20. They admired the scientist's (~~incite~~/insight) but said she was tired and should (~~lay~~/lie) down before the program.

21. At (~~about~~/around) 4 p.m. he dropped the (~~reigns~~/reins) as their (~~pray~~/prey), an elk, turned (its/~~it's~~) head, then ran (more than/~~over~~) a mile across the rough terrain.

Exercise 4. Verbs

SECTION I: AVOIDING USE OF NOUNS AS VERBS
1. She treated her own illness.
2. They flew to the site in a helicopter.
3. They are talking with their teacher.
4. They drove a truckload of furniture to their new home.
5. They were killed by blasts from a shotgun, and autopsies will be conducted Friday.

SECTION II: USING STRONGER VERBS
1. They bought (built/dug/obtained/ordered/received/won) a pool for their home.
2. About 800 students attend (go to/study at) the school.
3. The family's scrapbook contains (includes/provides/preserves) many photographs.
4. The book should contain (convey/offer/provide) more information about tennis.
5. The editor conducted (completed/directed/finished/supervised) a study of newsroom computerization.

SECTION III: USING STRONGER VERBS
1. The club needs more members.
2. Kathy Tijoriwalli owns the hot dog stand.
   SPELLING ERROR: The name Tijoriwalli (not Tijoriwali) is misspelled.
3. Miller testified that Paddock visited her three times.
4. A student threw a lemon meringue pie in the teacher's face.
5. The city pays for the summer recreation program.
6. To earn more money, she rents rooms in her house to three college students.
7. Good verbs can make stories more interesting.
8. A short circuit in the church's electrical wiring caused the fire.
9. The report said the mechanic failed to inspect the airplane's engine.
10. The article recommends that the appointment last only one year.

Exercise 5. Avoiding Common Errors

SECTION I: AVOIDING GRAMMATICAL AND VOCABULARY ERRORS
1. Rapists usually attack women **who** are vulnerable and alone.
2. The school board asked **its** attorney to help all the students **who** lost money.
3. Speaking for the highway patrol, Lucas said **it** would like larger and faster cars.
4. **Students** can do little to prevent cheating, except to cover **their** exam papers.

5.   The five men and three **women who** serve on the board predicted that the **number** of people seeking help at the clinic will grow to **about** 500 a month.

SECTION II: KEEPING RELATED WORDS AND IDEAS TOGETHER
1.   Her parents took the girl to a hospital for observation.
2.   The high school teachers honored 21 students, including two freshmen.
        SEXISM ISSUE: Should reporters use the word "freshman"? If not, what is a suitable alternative?
3.   The school board voted to ban from schools seven books that contain racist statements.
4.   After a high-speed chase, police arrested a suspect in the case, which involved the theft of two lawn mowers from a hardware store.
5.   Circuit Court Judge Samuel McGregor placed Robert Allen Wiess on probation after he pleaded guilty to violating probation.
        SPELLING ERROR: The name Wiess (not Wiese) is misspelled.

SECTION III: AVOIDING IMPRECISION
1.   People working in smaller grocery stores usually know their customers.
2.   After paying a $325 fine, its owner was free to take the dog home.
        SEXISM ISSUE: Students rewriting this sentence should avoid using the masculine "he" while referring to the dog's owner.
3.   A motorist stopped to help the accident victims, then called the police.
4.   A police officer saw a man fitting the description he had been given of the suspect.
5.   Minutes after the man left the bar, he destroyed his pickup truck in a collision with a car.
        NOTE: Students should avoid the redundancy "totally destroyed."

SECTION IV: DEFINING AND EXPLAINING
1.   Their son has meningitis, a disease that attacks the membranes surrounding the brain and spinal cord.
2.   A single B-2 Stealth bomber costs $800 million, an amount equal to the annual income of 60,000 residents of Mississippi.
3.   Pioneer 10, a satellite launched on March 2, 1972, is 4.2 billion miles from the sun, a distance greater than circling the Earth 168,803 times.

SECTION V: AVOIDING CLICHÉS
1.   The factory blaze spread from building to building.
2.   Automobile manufacturers strive to improve their cars to keep drivers interested.
3.   The woman handled the death of her grandfather well.
4.   The three inmates escaped in a compact car they stole from a used car lot.
5.   The senators faced a struggle in passing their legislation regarding student loans.

SECTION VI: AVOIDING UNNECESSARY PARENTHESES
1.   The mayor said she opposes any proposal to increase property taxes.
2.   Despite an estimated $4.2 million loss, he said the company should be able to pay all its debts before the Dec. 30 deadline.
3.   The governor predicted that the Legislature will approve the sales tax increase within 60 days.

SECTION VII: AVOIDING THE NEGATIVE
1.   She voted against raising property taxes.
2.   She received the $820 check in late August.
3.   The mayor said she may vote against the bill.
4.   The students may choose which songs they like.

5.   The restaurant is near.

SECTION VIII: IMPROVING SENTENCES
1.   He said it is a good book.
2.   The article added that most of today's most popular comedians are women.
3.   She said that before marijuana is legalized more research regarding its effects is needed.
4.   She wants to establish a program in which convicted juveniles can perform community service rather than be jailed.
5.   The latest fire occurred Sunday night in a basement room used by the school band, destroying 80 of its uniforms and causing an estimated $30,000 damage.

Exercise 6. Review

The textbook provides an answer key for students who complete this exercise. See Appendix D.

Exercise 7. Spelling and Vocabulary

The textbook provides an answer key for students who complete this exercise. See Appendix D.

Chapter 6. Basic News Leads

Exercise 1. Evaluating Good and Bad Leads

1. While this lead provides significant, newsworthy information, it could be written in the active voice rather than the passive voice.
    > A jury convicted a Baptist minister of drunken driving Tuesday after seeing a police video of his failed sobriety test.

    The second graph could identify the minister by name and note his sentence.
2. Vague lead that states the obvious. Every city police chief is concerned about crime.
3. Weak lead that does not focus on the news and begins with a long, vague prepositional phrase.
4. Lead provides details of council action, but could be rewritten to eliminate the opening prepositional phrase.
5. This lead is faulty because it is written in headline format. It fails to use proper sentence structure—subject, verb, object—or articles "the," "a" or "an."
6. Vague lead that provides no specific information on what kinds of animals are making the campus their home.
7. A clear, concise and specific lead that opens the story in such a way that the following paragraphs can build on the drama established by the lead.
8. A form of agenda lead, this lead fails to specify why this event is important or what is taking place. It merely orders readers to do something which may irritate them.
9. This lead is weak because it is vague. It should note the most important issue or issues the panel discussed. The lead also fails to mention specifics regarding the role of the press. Did the panel discuss the role of the press in society or in policy making or what?
10. This is a poor lead because it states the obvious. Every homecoming weak is filled with activities. The lead could mention the highlight of the week or an unusual event as a way of getting the readers' attention before covering other activities.
11. A good lead, but while it does state a consequential fact, it could be improved by indicating what governmental or other bureaucratic body is making the decision to bar guns.
12. This lead is poorly written and confusing. It reads as though the teen-age driver was paralyzed by the loss of control of the car rather than as a result of the car colliding with another vehicle or striking an object. One can be paralyzed by fear—a state of inaction—or one can be paralyzed as a result of injuries suffered in an accident—a physical disability. It is not clear in this lead which state affected the driver.
13. This lead is weak because it is written in passive voice and begins with the time element. In addition, it fails to note the important facts about the incident. If there was a shooting, was anyone injured or killed? It also uses the adjective "daring" to describe the robbery. Most readers would consider robbery a daring act and wouldn't have to be reminded of that fact.
14. A dull, routine lead that fails to mention specific advantages of the alternatives offered by the online courses.
15. A good two-sentence lead. It is specific and stresses the latest developments. One problem is the use of a parenthetical explanation of "adjuncts." It may be clearer and shorter to simply use the phrase "part-time faculty" rather than the term "adjuncts."
16. A dull, routine lead that fails to note specifics of the burglary. In addition, the lead is written in the passive voice.
17. While this lead gives specific details about what happened, it is a poor lead because the news is buried in the final brief sentence. The lead is choppy and omits other important details about the place, time and circumstances surrounding the death of the teen.

18.   A good two-sentence lead that provides specific details about the gang organization and its symbols.

Exercise 2. Leads

SECTION I. CONDENSING LENGTHY LEADS

1.   A 28-year-old woman was burned yesterday when sparks from her welder's torch started a fire that caused nearly $1 million in damage.
        SPELLING ERRORS: The names Maggy (not Maggie) and Baille (not Baile) are misspelled.
2.   The City Council last night voted 5-2 to require developers to construct sidewalks in front of every new home and in every new subdivision. (The lead should stress the news: the council's decision. Also, the lead should avoid stating the obvious: the fact that sidewalks are "for the convenience of pedestrians.")

SECTION II: USING THE PROPER SENTENCE STRUCTURE

1.   A judge today ordered a drunken driver who killed two teen-agers to seek professional help. The judge said it would not help anyone to imprison her.
2.   A 47-year-old was sentenced to six months in jail today for stabbing a man who contributed to his own death by refusing medical treatment.

SECTION III: EMPHASIZING THE NEWS

1.   Americans who practice "wellness" live 11 years longer than people who neglect their health, the secretary of Health and Human Services said today.
2.   Three members of a sorority at Iowa State University testified this morning that Steven House appeared drunk when he got into his car moments before it struck and killed a pedestrian.
        LOCALIZATION OPPORTUNITY: Students at Iowa State University can localize this lead.

SECTION IV: COMBINING MULTISENTENCE LEADS

1.   Detectives who posed as customers and employees captured two people who tried to rob a restaurant at 12:50 a.m. today.
2.   The mayor and her assistant resigned today after mechanics at the city garage complained that they were asked to repair, wash and wax the officials' private cars during work hours.

SECTION V: STRESSING THE UNUSUAL

1.   Last year police officer Daniel G. Silverbach was a hero. Now he's unemployed because his mustache is too long.
        FACTUAL ERROR: Silverbach's middle initial is G (not J).
2.   The state told a couple, married for a month, that they would be better off divorced . That's because Dale Snow, paralyzed in an accident, is no longer eligible for income benefits.
        FACTUAL ERROR: The Snows' address is 4381 (not 3418) Hazel St.
        ETHICAL ISSUE: Does anyone in your class object to use of the word "cripple"? If so, are there suitable alternatives?
3.   The ashes of nearly 50 percent of the people who are cremated when they die are never claimed. Now funeral directors want the state Legislature to tell them what to do with all those ashes.
4.   Dorothy R. Ellam buried her husband yesterday. At the same time, burglars were clearing out her home.
        FACTUAL ERROR: The correct address is 2481 Santana Blvd. (not Ave.)
        SEXISM ISSUE: Note the use of the word "repairmen."
        SPELLING ERROR: The name Ellam (not Elam) is misspelled.
5.   According to the local Social Security office, Gladies Ann Riggs is dead. That's news to her.

SPELLING ERRORS: The names Gladies (not Gladys) and Ann (not Anne) are misspelled.

SECTION VI: LOCALIZING YOUR LEAD
1. The state will widen Highway 17-92 from two to four lanes. Work is expected to begin in four months and take one and half years.
2. A local carpenter, his brother and sister-in-law were killed today when the plane in which they were riding crashed outside of Atlanta.
    FACTUAL ERROR: Skurow's first name is Melvin (not Melville)
    LOCALIZATION OPPORTUNITY: Students in Atlanta, Ga., can localize this lead.
3. Mayors from across the country selected Sabrina Datolli as first vice president at their annual convention.

SECTION VII: UPDATING YOUR LEAD
1. A man accused of murder said today he knew the victim.
    SPELLING ERROR: The name McDowell (not MacDowell) is misspelled.
2. A woman killed yesterday in a two-car crash was legally drunk, according to police today.
    SPELLING ERROR: The correct address is 1775 Nair (not Nairn) Drive.
    NOTE: The city director reveals that Brennan was director of the City Library.
3. A law which sets new restrictions on abortions goes into effect at midnight.

Exercise 3. Writing Basic News Leads (Pro Challenge)

1. A fire engine responding to a false alarm collided with a van today, killing its driver and sending two firefighters to a hospital.

    By Eric Dentel

    A man was killed and two firefighters were hospitalized this morning when a van collided with a fire engine responding to what turned out to be a false alarm.

    By Loraine O'Connell

    SPELLING ERROR: The name Lydin (not Lydon or Lyden) was spelled inconsistently.
    SEXISM ISSUE: Should reporters use the word "firemen"?

2. Larger automobiles are safer, a Highway Loss Data Institute study has found.

    By Eric Dentel

    When it comes to cars, bigger is safer, according to an auto insurance industry report issued today.

    By Loraine O'Connell

3. Hot dogs can be deadly to young children, and other common foods — candy, nuts, grapes, carrots and more — can be dangerous to those under age 10.

    By Eric Dentel

    Hot dogs are a health hazard — especially for children under age 4.

    By Loraine O'Connell

4. Christine Belcuor's family buried a stranger last week.

    By Eric Dentel

More than 100 friends and relatives attended the closed-casket funeral of Christine Belcuor last Saturday. Today, the grieving family learned that the body they buried was not that of Belcuor.

By Loraine O'Connell

SPELLING ERRORS: The names Christine (not Kristine) and Belcuor (not Belcuore) are misspelled.

5. Lifestyle changes, not graduate degrees, make highly educated women more prone to divorce, according to an Ohio State University sociologist's study.

By Eric Dentel

Women who want a graduate degree and a husband should get their master's degrees before their marriage certificates, a study says.

By Loraine O'Connell

6. Gun-control laws do nothing to prevent career criminals, but they may have some positive effects, a Justice Department study has found.

By Eric Dentel

Gun-control laws do nothing to prevent career criminals from getting weapons. That information comes straight from the horses' mouths: 1,874 convicted felons questioned by the Department of Justice.

By Loraine O'Connell

7. Thomas C. Ahl avoided the death penalty, but the 24-year-old murderer of two restaurant employees will be 89 before he is eligible for parole.

By Eric Dentel

A man who pleaded guilty to killing two restaurant employees today received the longest sentence ever handed down in this state.

By Loraine O'Connell

8. A group of acoustics experts says that if noise levels continue to increase, everyone living in a city could be deaf by 2020.

By Eric Dentel

The world's noise levels are rising, and if the increase continues, "everyone living in cities could be stone-deaf by the year 2020."

By Loraine O'Connell

9. Police will not charge a bystander whose restraint of a struggling shoplifting suspect lead to the suspect's death.

By Eric Dentel

Police today said they don't plan to charge anyone in the death of a 19-year-old shoplifting suspect, calling his death "a case of excusable homicide."

By Loraine O'Connell

SPELLING ERROR: The name Millan (not Milan) is misspelled.

10. Huck Finn will be allowed into local junior high libraries, but not classrooms, Superintendent Gary Hubbard announced today.

By Eric Dentel

Junior high school students no longer will be required to read "The Adventures of Huckleberry Finn." And high school teachers who assign the book will have some explaining to do — about historical setting and social context.

By Loraine O'Connell

Exercise 4. Campus Stories (Pro Challenge)

1. A professor who burned an American flag, prompting 250 protesters to sing the national anthem outside her classroom this morning, will not be punished, the school's president said.

By Geoffrey M. Giordano

Scores of students marched, chanted and sang the national anthem on campus today to protest the burning of an American flag by a professor who said she was teaching a lesson in free speech.

By Dana Eagles

SPELLING ERROR: The name Bealle (not Beall) is misspelled.

2. Students circulating a petition opposed to the first lady's speaking at spring commencement will meet with the school's president Friday to air their grievance.

By Geoffrey M. Giordano

Having the first lady speak at commencement would be honoring a woman for her husband instead of her achievement, according to more than 300 students who have petitioned the university to withdraw the invitation.

By Dana Eagles

SEXISM ISSUE: The story uses the masculine "he" while referring to the president of your school. Yet some schools, perhaps yours, have female presidents, and students at those schools should correct the error.

3. Women in their first year of higher education are nearly three times as likely to gain weight as women who don't attend college, a school dietitian says.

By Geoffrey M. Giordano

Freshmen are likely to gain more than wisdom as they adjust to college life — namely, 10 or 15 pounds.

By Dana Eagles

SPELLING ERROR: The word dietitian (not dietician) is misspelled.

4. Investments in tobacco companies made by the university foundation should stand, the Board of Regents voted today.

By Geoffrey M. Giordano

The university foundation may continue to invest in tobacco companies despite the health risks of cigarettes, the Board of Regents decided today.

By Dana Eagles

5. Nearly one in 10 female university students has had an abortion, some as early as age 12, campus medical researchers have found.

By Geoffrey M. Giordano

One in 10 women on campus has had an abortion, and some had them as early as age 12, a student clinic survey has found.

By Dana Eagles

6. A fraternity faces disciplinary action after five members were arrested following a hazing incident Friday that hospitalized two students.

By Geoffrey M. Giordano

Five members of Sigma Kappa Chi fraternity were arrested after two pledges were hospitalized with injuries suffered in a Friday hazing incident, police said.

By Lisa Lochridge

SEXISM ISSUE: Note the use of the word "spokesman."
SPELLING ERRORS: The names Desaur (not Dessaur) and Eddy (not Eddie) are misspelled.

Exercise 5. City, State and National Leads (Pro Challenge)

CITY BEAT

1. A restaurant where a mouse jumped on a city inspector and where food was stored in a janitor's closet had its license suspended late yesterday.

By Geoffrey M. Giordano

Calling a restaurant "an immediate threat to public health," the city suspended its license yesterday after one mouse ran across the dining room and another jumped on a health official during an inspection.

By Lisa Lochridge

2. The school district reached a settlement today with a Colonial High School biology student who refused to dissect animals, saying the practice violated her religious beliefs.

By Geoffrey M. Giordano

A Colonial High School biology student who refused to dissect animals because of religious beliefs will have her failing grade changed to a "B" after the School Board agreed today to settle a lawsuit brought by her parents.

By Lisa Lochridge

3. An orthodontist infected with the AIDS virus has mailed letters to more than 5,000 patients, urging them to be tested in the unlikely event he spread the disease through his practice.

By Mike Griffin

After learning he has AIDS, an orthodontist who has treated almost 6,000 patients during his career closed his practice today.

By Lisa Lochridge

FACTUAL ERROR: Leforge's first name is Ted (not Todd).
SPELLING ERROR: The name Leforge (not Lefforge) is misspelled.

4. A man facing burglary charges could be a suspect in hundreds of break-ins in the past year, police said last night.

By Mike Griffin

A man charged with burglary and grand theft said he found that stealing and reselling jewelry and coins was more profitable than holding down a job.

By Lisa Lochridge

FACTUAL ERROR: Johnson's address is 2643 (not 2463) Pioneer Road.
SPELLING ERROR: The names Johnson (not Johnsen) and Marc (not Mark) are misspelled.

5. Gusting crosswinds likely contributed to the crash of a single-engine plane at the airport, officials said.

By Mike Griffin

A pilot and three passengers escaped serious injury yesterday when their wind-tossed airplane crashed at the airport during landing exercises.

By Lisa Lochridge

FACTUAL ERROR: Fowler's address is 2006 (not 2606) Hillcrest St.

STATE BEAT

1. A proposed law that would force newspaper opinion writers to sign their editorials is attracting support in the state Senate and criticism from the State Press Association.

By Mike Griffin

Saying newspaper editorial writers should be "accountable to their readers," state Sen. Neil Iacobi said today he is drafting a bill requiring writers' signatures on editorials.

By Lisa Lochridge

SEXISM ISSUE: Should students use the word "newspapermen" while referring to both men and women?
SPELLING ERROR: The name DiLorrento (not DiLorento) is misspelled.

2. Disposable diapers would disappear from the state by Jan. 1 under a bill introduced in the state Senate today.

By Eric Dentel

Banning disposable diapers will clean up the environment, according to a state senator, but opponents argue the measure would lead to unhealthy conditions at day care centers.

By Mike Griffin

SEXISM ISSUE: The story calls a woman a "spokesman."
SPELLING ERROR: The name Simmens (not Simmons) is spelled inconsistently.

3. More state prisoners are women, and more are elderly, causing problems for the Department of Corrections, the department's head testified today.

By Eric Dentel

Record numbers of women and elderly inmates in state prisons are straining the medical services and facilities of a system designed for young men, the state's top jailer told legislators today.

By Mike Griffin

4. Check bouncers will face stiffer penalties under a law signed by the governor today.

By Eric Dentel

Stiff new penalties aimed at taking the bounce out of bad checks won praise from merchants today.

By Mike Griffin

5. The state's Outstanding Teacher today criticized part-time jobs for high school students, saying they leave pupils little time to learn.

By Eric Dentel

Students spending too much time flipping burgers and running cash registers are jeopardizing their future, said the state's top teacher, who dubbed minimum wage jobs "the silent killers of quality education."

By Mike Griffin

SPELLING ERROR: The name Younge (not Young) is misspelled.

NATIONAL BEAT

1. Almost a tenth of American adults who grew up speaking English are illiterate in their native language, the Census Bureau reported today.

By Dana Eagles

Illiteracy in the United States is highest among adults for whom English is a second language, the Census Bureau said today.

By Loraine O'Connell

2. Americans are drinking less hard liquor than at any time since 1959, and consumption of all alcoholic beverages is dropping, a federal agency reported Friday.

By Dana Eagles

Americans' consumption of hard liquor has plunged to its lowest level since 1959, the Centers for Disease Control said Friday.

By Loraine O'Connell

3. The House of Representatives approved a $2 billion increase in the nation's space budget today but cut $12 million the president wanted to listen for radio signals from aliens.

By Dana Eagles

The House today rejected the president's $12 million program designed to search for extraterrestrial intelligence.

By Loraine O'Connell

LOCALIZATION OPPORTUNITY: Students in Rhode Island can localize this lead.

4.   The Department of Veterans Affairs today admitted that it has been paying almost $6 million a year to more than 1,200 dead veterans.

By Dana Eagles

Sometimes you can take it with you.
     The Department of Veterans Affairs said today that it has been paying benefits to more than 1,200 veterans who are dead, at a cost of about $5.7 million a year. About 100 of the veterans have been dead a decade or more.

By Loraine O'Connell

5.   Home ownership is declining among young families as high rents make it hard to save a down payment, a trade association survey has found.

By Dana Eagles

The home ownership rate among families in the 25-to-34 age group has fallen to 45 percent — and prospects for an upturn look bleak, a survey shows.

By Loraine O'Connell

LOCALIZATION OPPORTUNITY: Students in Las Vegas can localize this lead.

Chapter 7. Alternative Leads

Exercise 1. Evaluating Alternative Leads

1. An effective two-paragraph lead: clear and specific, and it introduces both sides of a controversial issue.
2. A good question lead: short, clear and provocative.
3. A good descriptive lead until the last sentence which is a bit over dramatic. Use either "Immediately," or "Right then," but not both. Many beginning writers repeat phrases for emphasis, but tend to over dramatize something by doing so.
4. The lead is vague and does not explain to the reader why retirement may be harmful.
5. An effective two-sentence lead that sets the scene for the rest of the story.
6. An ineffective question lead that fails to draw the reader into the story.
7. This lead might be effective if it did not border on a cliché. The phrase "It's (whatever time), do you know where your (children, pets, parents, etc.) are?" has been used to the point of becoming a cliché.
8. A good descriptive lead with a twist at the end. Without giving away the suspect's identity, the weight (715 pounds) at the end of the description startles readers and entices them to read on to discover the suspect's identity.
9. A good buried lead that provides details that draw reader into the story.
10. This would be a better question lead if it did not rely on a cliche. However, it does provide specific information about the council's action.
11. This lead uses quotes effectively, but would benefit from a better transitional sentence at the end. The last sentence of the lead is a bit routine and could be improved.
12. While this lead uses partial quotes effectively, it is vague and fails to mention the specific action for which the petition was signed.
13. An effective lead that uses both description and quotations to introduce the topic.
14. A good descriptive lead. Note the effective use of short, repetitive words in the opening sentence to create the often chaotic sounds and scene of a construction site.
15. An effective question lead that draws the reader into the story.
16. This lead is based on an often-used and tired formula — that of the sheriff (or deputy, marshal, police officer, etc.) hanging up his or her gun and riding into the sunset.

Exercise 2. Writing Alternative Leads

1. **LOCALIZATION OPPORTUNITY:** Students in the Midwest could localize this story to indicate that their areas are less expensive to raise children.
2. A good opportunity for students to write an ironic lead.
3. **SPELLING ERROR:** The name Melba Novogreski (not Melbi Novogroski) is misspelled.
4. **LOCALIZATION OPPORTUNITY:** Students in the Southwest could localize this story to emphasize the effect on small lizard populations. **NOTE:** "Kitties" is slang or a colloquialism for cats or felines.
5. A good opportunity to write an ironic or buried lead.
6. A good opportunity to write a quotation lead. **NOTE:** There are a number of style errors including the need to abbreviate "Lieutenant" and spelling out "percent" (not %) in the story.

Exercise 3. Pro Challenge

The following leads are written by reporters for The Orlando Sentinel.

1.   Police looking for a bank robber lifted the lid of the trash bin behind McDonald's and found something unexpected: McSuspect.

     SPELLING ERROR: The name Allen (not Alan) is misspelled.
     FACTUAL ERRORS: The correct address is Apartment 322 (not 223) at 840 (not 820) Apollo Drive.

2.   No cake, no dress, no hugs — not even a kiss.
     They weren't allowed.
     A county judge married Sunni McGrath and her fiance in court Monday — minutes after sentencing the woman to a year's probation for drunken driving. As soon as she said "I do," the bride was ordered back to prison, where she is serving time for other crimes.

3.   When Michael Uosis heard someone banging at a window of his home early today, he thought it was the man who had robbed him a few weeks ago, coming back to rob him again. Uosis got out his .38-caliber revolver and fired a shot at the window.
     It wasn't a robber. It was Edward Beaumont, Uosis' friend and former fellow worker. Beaumont, 40, was shot in the head and may be paralyzed.

4.   A burglary went stale today when a janitor surprised two intruders at a VFW post and pummeled them with two old loaves of bread and a box of stale rolls.
     The teen-agers dropped part of the loot and ran to avoid more bun beating.

     SPELLING ERROR: The name Stephen (not Steven) is misspelled.

5.   Troy Dysart was looking for a car to steal Tuesday morning.
     At 8:30 a.m. he found his target, parked at the door of Albertsons at 4240 Michigan St., with the keys in the ignition.
     But Dysart, 21, neglected to follow an important rule: "Make sure you don't get more than you bargained for."
     Dysart said he was "moving too fast" to see 4-year-old Troy Sodergreen and his 8-month-old sister, Jena, who were in the car as he pulled out of Albertsons.
     "I saw the keys and got in but I didn't notice the kids. When I turn around the corner I looked to my side and saw the little girl lying on the seat," Dysart said.
     "I saw the kids and say, 'Oh, damn.' I freaked out and parked the car...."

     ETHICAL ISSUES: Should reporters change or delete the word "damn"? Also, should they correct Dysart's grammatical errors?

Chapter 8. The Body of a News Story

Exercise 1. The Body of a News Story

SECTION I: SECOND PARAGRAPHS

1. Grade: C. Transition fails to identify James as the courier.
2. Grade: D. The second paragraph does not continue with the central point developed in the lead. The fact Alvarez has worked at the school for 21 years is irrelevant to her lawsuit.
3. Grade: B. The second paragraph lets readers know important information, but that information may be broadcast before the next edition of the newspaper appears.
4. Grade: F. The second paragraph is filled with routine information that does little to advance the story. Readers will want to know how and why the shooting happened, not that emergency personnel responded—that is a given fact.
5. Grade: B. A good lead, but the transition fails to identify Howland as the 32-year-old woman mentioned in the lead.
6. Grade: C. Readers might want to know Deacosti's reaction or a bit more about the robbery rather than the fact that Deacosti was on duty.
7. Grade: A. A good second paragraph that tells the reader something about the subject of the story.
8. Grade: A. This second paragraph is filled with description about the incident.

SECTION II: TRANSITIONS

1. Grade: B. A good transition that provides the other side of an issue. **NOTE:** This sentence could be improved with the addition of the transitional word "however" at the beginning.
2. Grade: A. This transition effectively uses a question to carry the reader into the next part of the story.
3. Grade: F. A vague transition that fails to give any news or build on the preceding information.
4. Grade: C. The transition is rather ordinary. While it serves as a bridge between two separate ideas, it fails to tell the reader anything newsworthy.
5. Grade: A. A good transition that provides readers with details about the incident.
6. Grade: D. This transition fails to tell readers what Hubbard's concerns are.
7. Grade: A. A good transition that continues the story and provides the reader with Kopperud's reaction. **NOTE:** Chief should be capitalized.
8. Grade: F. Routine transition that fails to mention why or how prejudice is a problem.
9. Grade: D. Transition fails to note what she said about the celebrations and rituals.
10. Grade: A. good transition that effectively builds on previous information.

Exercise 2. Writing Complete Stories (Pro Challenge)

1. By Mike Griffin

While workers run the assembly line in General Electric's new plant, their children could be attending school right there at the factory, under a program School Board members approved last night.

The district and the company are still negotiating the details, but the plans call for GE to build three classrooms for 60 kindergarten and first-grade children, School Superintendent Gary Hubbard said. The district would spend $30,000 equipping the rooms and will hire three teachers and three aides to instruct the students.

Board members voted 6-1 for the plan that Hubbard said made both sides winners.

Because the school would be on-site, single parents could drop their children off before their shift, pick them up at the end of the day and even eat lunch with them in the company's cafeteria.

GE gets happier employees, reduces its turnover and saves money training new employees.

If it works, the School Board will set up classrooms at other companies, reducing crowding in some schools, Hubbard said.

But the program, being tried in 20 districts through the country, won't work for all companies. At least 20 children must be enrolled for the program to be cost-effective, Hubbard said.

GE's new plant will employ 600 people, many of them on the assembly line, and Hubbard said those workers are less likely to be late, to be fired or quit their jobs if they have more time to spend with their children.

FACTUAL ERROR: Hubbard's first name is Gary (not Greg).

2. By Geoffrey M. Giordano
A posse of shoppers turned in a sparkling anti-crime effort last night, chasing a thief into the parking lot of Colonial Mall and holding him for police.

Shortly before the mall closed at 10 p.m., a man used a hammer to smash two display cases at Elaine's Jewelry. As the man scooped up handfuls of rings and watches, store owner Elaine Blanchfield began screaming.

Enter the cavalry.

Witnesses say eight to 10 shoppers chased the thief as he fled the store with a bag of loot. The crowd, screaming at the man, grew as the chase proceeded into the parking lot, where the thief threw down his bag of loot.

Finally, Asa Smythe, who says he jogs 20 miles a week, caught up with and tackled the thief.

"He couldn't lose me, no way he could lose me," said Smythe, a former high school football player and Marine.

Barbara Keith-Fowler, the first police officer to reach the scene, said the suspect seemed glad to see her. About 20 shoppers surrounded the thief, threatening him while shaking hands among themselves and applauding their good deed.

"Things like that just make me mad," said Keith Holland, one of the shoppers who pursued the thief.

As the thief stood cornered, a bystander retrieved the bag of goods and returned it to Blanchfield.

Blanchfield later said her helpers are "a super bunch of people who make me feel wonderful." She thinks they responded because they are tired of people being victimized.

Todd Burnes, 23, of 1502 Matador Drive, Apt. 203, was charged with grand theft. Burnes, a police officer, is being held at County Jail on $25,000 bail.

FACTUAL ERROR: The correct apartment number is 203 (not 302).
SPELLING ERRORS: The names Blanchfield (not Benchfield, Blanchfeld or Blancfield) and Burnes (not Burns) are spelled inconsistently.
NOTE: The city directory reveals that Burnes is a police officer, a fact that students should include in their stories and probably higher up than in the example given.

3. By Geoffrey M. Giordano
Someone wants to throw cold water on a hot circus act — Sandra Kidder's flaming-hoop defying "Fabulous Flying Felines."

These uncommon kitties, with their jumps through rings of fire, have been a favorite at the Shriners' annual circus since it opened here Friday night.

But Annette Daigel of 431 E. Central Blvd. and others concerned for the cats' well-being are in dogged opposition to the animals' antics, and Daigel has filed a complaint with the Humane Society.

The cats are forced to perform unnaturally, Daigel says, and the last thing they want to do is go near fire. Daigel says Kidder terrorizes and starves the cats to get them to jump through the hoops.

Rene Chung-Peters, director of the Humane Society, says she is investigating the complaint and hopes to examine the cats up close after their nightly performance.

Kidder says Daigel's claims are hogwash.

Kidder of Farmers Branch, Texas, says she feeds her cats one good meal a day. She feeds them after the show, she says, because otherwise they might fall asleep in the middle of their performance, in which they leap from stool to stool, stand on their hind legs and sit on their haunches, appearing to beg as dogs do.

She acknowledges that it is unnatural for the cats to stand on their hind legs, but explains that they do it for her because she loves them and they love her.

Also, she says it is easier for her cats to learn to jump through fire than to master many of their other tricks.

The cats are not afraid of the flaming hoops, Kidder says; they are afraid only if someone is mean to them.

Kidder's shining stars have rather humble origins; some came from a pound, others from friends.

She says she welcomes Chung-Peters' plans to get a closer look at her cats, which will perform every night at 8 until the circus ends Saturday.

ETHICAL ISSUE: In this age of sensitivity, should reporters call the children "retarded"?
SPELLING ERROR: The names Daigel (not Daigle or Diagle) and Rene (not Renee) are misspelled.
LOCALIZATION OPPORTUNITY: Students in Texas, especially the Dallas area, can localize this lead.

4. By Lisa Lochridge

Hundreds of members and employees of six Mr. Muscles health spas were surprised Wednesday morning to find the workout centers had closed without warning.

Those who showed up at the spas at 6 a.m. found notices taped to the locked doors saying, "Closed until further notice."

Some of the company's 180 employees worried about whether they would get their biweekly paycheck today, which is payday. The company had given them no hint it was in financial trouble, they said.

The state Department of Consumer Affairs is investigating the closing of the spas owned by Mike Cantrell, 410 South St. The state attorney's office also is investigating.

Cantrell was unavailable for comment.

It is unlikely the spas' approximately 12,000 members would get refunds, Consumer Affairs Director Kim Eng said. Some members paid up to $499 a year, and an undetermined number of members had paid $3,999 for lifetime memberships.

Sales of memberships had fallen in recent months, leaving the company unable to pay its bills, said Jena Cruz, Cantrell's attorney.

Cruz said she doesn't expect the company, which has operated in the city for more than 15 years to reopen. The clubs have been losing about $3,000 a week and have been unable to make loan payments, Cruz said.

She said the company plans to file for bankruptcy in federal court next week.

Mr. Muscles, the area's largest chain of spas, opened its first workout center in 1981. The company borrowed heavily to build the six spas, each of which cost more than $1 million to build and equip, Cruz said.

SPELLING ERROR: The name Cantrell (not Cantral) is misspelled.

5. By Dana Eagles

A 7-year-old girl whose tonsils were removed at Mercy Hospital died Saturday after a nurse gave her a stronger pain reliever than ordered, hospital officials said today.

The nurse who administered the drug to Tania Abbondanzio has been suspended until the hospital's investigation is complete. Hospital officials did not identify her.

The hospital gave this account of the girl's death, which police investigators are regarding as accidental:

Tania, the daughter of Anthony and Deborah Abbondanzio of 473 Geele Ave., was admitted to Mercy Hospital on Friday and had a tonsillectomy that morning. Her physician, Dr. Priscilla Eisen, prescribed a half a milligram of a pain reliever called morphine sulphate after surgery. But at 2:30 p.m. Friday, a pediatric nurse instead gave the girl a half milligram of hydromorphone, a stronger narcotic commonly known as Dilaudid.

Ten minutes later, Tania developed breathing problems, then complained of being hot and had an apparent seizure. She was placed in intensive care and remained in a coma until Saturday morning, when doctors pronounced her brain-dead. She was removed from a respirator and died at 9:40 a.m.

A weekend autopsy confirmed the hospital's explanation of Tania's death.

"Our sympathy goes out to the family, and we will stay close to them to provide support," said Dr. Irwin Greenhouse, the hospital's administrator. Tania's parents were not available for comment.

The two pain relievers are kept side by side in a locked cabinet at the hospital. The nurse discovered her error during a routine narcotics inventory at midnight Friday and immediately told her supervisor.

Hospital officials said hydromorphone is six or seven times more potent than morphine sulphate but that a half milligram of the stronger drug is not normally considered lethal, even for a child.

A pharmacist who spoke on the condition that she not be identified agreed that the dosage seems reasonable. She said children sometimes are given a half milligram of hydromorphone to control coughing.

ETHICAL ISSUE: Should students quote anonymous sources, such as the pharmacist who does not want to be identified?

SPELLING ERROR: The name Abbondanzio (not Abondanzio nor Abbondanzia) is misspelled.

6. By Lee Fritz

A small device, disguised to look like a packet of money, exploded in a bank robber's pickup truck yesterday, apparently spraying the robber, his truck and money with red dye.

"The guy should be covered with red. The money, too. Just look for a red man with red money," Detective Myron A. Neely said.

"You can't wash that stuff off," Neely explained. "It explodes all over the place — in your clothes, in your hair, on your hands, in your car. It's almost like getting in contact with a skunk."

Police and bank officials gave this account of the robbery:

The man entered Security Federal Bank at 814 N. Main St. at about 2:30 p.m., talked to a loan officer, then left. The man returned a few minutes later, brandishing a pistol and demanding money from the bank's tellers.

The gunman forced two tellers to lie on the floor, then jumped behind a counter and scooped up the money in five cash drawers. As he scooped up the money, the gunman also scooped up the device filled with red dye and tear gas. The device explodes after being taken from a bank.

As the gunman left, he ordered four customers to lie on the floor. Until then, most were unaware of the robbery.

The man had left his pickup truck in a parking lot behind the bank and police found a red stain on the pavement there. They surmise that the device exploded as the robber was getting into the truck.

Moments after the robbery, a witness reported seeing a red cloud coming out the window of a late-model black pickup truck a few blocks away.

An FBI agent said the dye will remain on the man for at least the next two or three days and will remain on the money forever.

The robber was a white male, 25 to 30 years old. He is about 6 feet tall, weighs about 180 pounds and has long blond hair. He wore wire-rimmed sunglasses, a gold wedding ring, blue plaid shirt, blue jeans and brown sandals.

SPELLING ERRORS: The names Gladies (not Gladys) and Neely (not Neeley) are misspelled.

Exercise 3. Writing Complete News Stories

1. **SPELLING ERROR:** Jabil's first name is Stephen (not Steven).
    ETHICAL ISSUE: Should the complete address of the girl be given in this case or should her parents also be identified in the story?

2. **SPELLING ERRORS:** The names Kopperud (not Koperud), Nouse (not Noruse), Amanpor (not Amanpour) and Linn (not Lin) are misspelled.
    SEXISM ISSUE: Story identifies two witnesses as Mr. and Mrs. Elton Amanpor rather than as Elton and Effie Amanpor.

5. **SPELLING ERROR:** The name Herrin (not Herron) is misspelled.

Exercise 4. Reporting Controversial Stories

2. **SPELLING ERRORS:** The names Shadgott (not Shadgett), Lasiter (not Lasater) and Perakiss (not Perakis) are misspelled.
    SEXISM ISSUE: Should students use the word "statesmen," which appears in a direct quotation? Should students use the word if they paraphrase the quotation?
    ETHICAL ISSUE: Is there a particular need to use Onn's middle name (Chinn) rather than just the middle initial? Using the name may identify the victim's race which is not necessary for the story and it takes up unnecessary space.

3. **ETHICAL ISSUE:** Should students use Wong's quote: "It's a hell of a mess"?
    FACTUAL ERROR: Hubbard's first name is Gary (not Greg), and Wong's first name is Steven (not Stephen).

Chapter 9. Quotations and Attribution

Exercise 1. Improving Quotations and Attribution

SECTION I: AVOIDING DOUBLE ATTRIBUTION
1. The U.S. Department of Justice reported Tuesday that the number of serious crimes committed in the United States declined 3 percent last year.
2. She told more than 3,000 people in the Municipal Auditorium that only the Democratic Party favors universal health care.
3. Last year, 5.2 million people in the United States, including 620,000 children, were homeless, the Census Bureau reported today.

SECTION II: CORRECTING PLACEMENT ERRORS
1. People under 18 should not be allowed to drive, she said.
2. She said another important step is to lower the books' prices.
3. "The average shoplifters are teen-age girls who steal for the thrill of it, and housewives who steal items they can use," Valderama said. "They don't have to steal; most have plenty of money, but they don't think it's a crime. They also think they'll get away with it forever."
    SPELLING ERROR: The name Valderama (not Valderrama) is misspelled.

SECTION III: CONDENSING WORDY ATTRIBUTION
1. She said the jamboree will be held from Aug. 7 to 13. Or: She told the scouts that the jamboree will be held from Aug. 7 to 13.
2. He said the president has "failed to act effectively to reduce the federal deficit."
3. She said that all those convicted of drunken driving should lose their licenses for life.
4. She added that federal studies show that recycling 1 ton of paper can save 17 trees. (Be careful to avoid second-person pronouns in news stories, unless they are in direct quotations.)
5. In a speech Tuesday, he told the students that their professors should emphasize teaching, not research.
6. He said the country's energy policy has failed: The United States is neither developing alternative fuels nor conserving existing fuels.

SECTION IV: IMPROVING ATTRIBUTION
1. He said, "After a certain number of years, our faces become our biographies." (Use a comma after the attribution. Capitalize the first word in direct quotations that are a complete sentence. Place the period inside the final quotation mark.)
2. Andy Rooney declared, "If dogs could talk, it would take a lot of fun out of owning one." (Place a comma after the attribution. Capitalize the first word in quotations that are a complete sentence. Place the period inside the quotation mark.)
3. When asked why he robbed banks, Willie Sutton answered, "Because that's where the money is." (Place the explanation before, not after, the quotation, and place a comma after the attribution.)
4. He said there are two types of people who complain about their taxes: men and women. (Condense the attribution and eliminate the orphan quotes. Because most of the sentence is an indirect quotation, students cannot place quotation marks around the entire sentence.)
5. W.C. Bennett said, "Blessed is he who expects no gratitude, for he shall not be disappointed." (The attribution should use normal word order and should appear at the beginning or end of the quotation, or at a natural break in the quotation. Place a comma after the attribution. Attribute a direct quotation only once, and place the period inside the quotation mark.)
6. Mother Teresa told the youths, "The most terrible poverty is loneliness and the feeling of being

unwanted." (Condense the attribution, avoiding its redundancy. Place a comma, not a period, after the attribution. Don't use "that" before a full sentence of direct quotation.)

7. Robert F. Kennedy said, "My views on birth control are somewhat distorted by the fact that I was the seventh of nine children." (Place the attribution at the beginning or end of the quotation or at a natural break in the quotation. The attribution should use normal word order. Place the period inside the quotation mark.)

8. Being a police officer is not always fun and exciting, Griffin says. "Some things you'd just as soon forget," she explained. "Some things you do forget." (The attribution should use the normal word order. Clearly attribute the direct quotation.)
   SEXISM ISSUE: While attributing the sentence, students should not assume that Griffin is a man. The city directory reveals that Griffin is a woman.
   SPELLING ERROR: The name Griffin (not Griffith) is misspelled.

9. A French statesman long ago said, "The art of taxation consists in so plucking the goose as to obtain the most feathers with the least hissing." (The attribution should use normal word order. Avoid "claimed" as a word of attribution. Place the attribution at the beginning or end of the quotation. Capitalize only the first word of the quoted sentence. Place the period inside the quotation mark.)
   SEXISM ISSUE: Note the use of the word "statesman."

10. Dr. Hector Rivera said they test for AIDS at the clinic but do not treat the disease. "People come in to be tested scared to death," he said. "Some leave the clinic relieved, and some don't." (Avoid partial quotations. Attribute every direct quotation once. Put the attribution at the beginning or at the first natural break in a long quotation.)

11. The most important things in her life are her friendships, home and family. "My husband is my best friend," she said. "Maybe that's why we've lasted so long. You really need to be friends before you're lovers." (Place the explanation before, not after, a list. Clearly attribute the direct quotation — and near the beginning, not end, of the quotation. Place quotation marks only at the beginning and end of a direct quotation, not at the beginning and end of every sentence in the quotation. Place the final period inside the quotation mark.)

12. The history major said he cheats and has never been caught. He cheats, he said, because professors assign too much work. "They don't take into consideration that some people have jobs, families and outside interests," he continued. (Condense the attribution. Students may also want to paraphrase and simplify portions of the direct quotation. Identify the source earlier in the quotation.)

13. "My son thinks I'm old," he said. "But I'm actually in good health for my age. Of course, I have the usual aches and pains of an 80-year-old. But I can still take care of my own house, and I still enjoy it. My son thinks I should move into one of those retirement apartments and watch 'Wheel of Fortune' all day." (Place the attribution earlier in the quotation: at the beginning or end of the first sentence. Place quotation marks only at the beginning and end of a direct quotation, not at the beginning and end of every sentence in the quotation. The attribution should use normal word order.)

14. JoAnne Nyer, a secretary, grew up in Milwaukee and described a childhood fear: A house that was at the end of her street and that no one would dare go near on Halloween. She said it was supposed to be haunted. People thought the wife had hanged herself in the basement and that the husband killed and ate rattlesnakes, she explained. (Because the quotation is a paraphrase, students cannot place even a portion of the quotation in quotation marks. The entire quotation may be a reporter's summary, not the source's exact words)
   SPELLING ERRORS: The names JoAnne (not Jo Ann) and Nyer (not Nyez) are misspelled.
   NOTE: Use "hanged," not "hung," as the past tense verb to describe a suicide.

Exercise 2. Wording, Placement and Punctuation

The textbook provides an answer key for students who complete this exercise. See Appendix D.

Exercise 3. Using Quotes in News Stories

1.   **LOCALIZATION OPPORTUNITY**: Students in Tennessee can localize this lead.
        SPELLING ERROR: The name Vacanti (not Vacante) is misspelled.

Exercise 4. Using Quotes in News Stories

1.   **SPELLING ERROR**: The name Layous (not Layoux) is misspelled.
        ETHICAL ISSUE: The story uses the trade name "Winston" cigarettes. Should students use that trade name in their stories? Is it important and relevant — and fair to the manufacturer to associate its product with an armed robbery?
2.   **SPELLING ERROR**: The name Shisenauntt (not Shisenaunt) is misspelled.

Chapter 10. Interviews

Exercise 3. Interview With a Robbery Victim

ETHICAL ISSUE: Should students identify this college student? The student has not told her parents about the incident and says, "They would be very angry that I fought back." Is her name important to the story? Or, did the student waive her right to privacy while giving the interview? Also, should students polish the source's quotes, eliminating her grammatical errors and phrases such as "you know"?

Exercise 6. Hospital Bill

ETHICAL ISSUE: Should students use the words "damn" and "hell" in their stories? Should they polish the source's direct quotations, eliminating words such as "uh" and "ya"?

Chapter 11. Writing Obituaries

Exercise 1. Writing Obituaries

BLACKFOOT OBITUARY
FACT ERROR: Blackfoot is survived by her husband Jason (not Johnny).
ETHICAL ISSUES: Do you need to mention that Blackfoot's son was adopted? Is it necessary to include that Blackfoot was ill for five weeks and with breast cancer?
FACT ERROR and NOTE: The street Wendover (not Wentover) is misspelled. Should a reporter include the address?

SHEPARD OBITUARY
ETHICAL ISSUES: Should reporters mention in an obituary that Shepard died "of symptoms brought about by the ingestion of a large quantity of cocaine"? Also, should journalists list her roommate among her survivors?
SPELLING ERROR: The name Bolanker (not Bolankner) is misspelled.
FACT ERROR and NOTE: The street Murray (not Maury) is misspelled. Should the address appear in the obituary?

Exercise 2. Writing Obituaries

OBITUARY NOTICE: AUSTIN
SPELLING ERRORS: The names Terrance (not Terrence) and Deacosti (not Deacosta) are misspelled.
ETHICAL ISSUES: Should reporters include Anna Austin's remark that her husband smoked two or more packs of cigarettes a day and that is what killed him?

OBITUARY NOTICE: CAPIELLO
SPELLING ERROR: The name Ann (not Anne) is spelled inconsistently.
ETHICAL ISSUES: Should reporters say before or after an autopsy that a person died of apparent suicide and from an overdose of prescription drugs? Is it important to include where the body was found and that it is awaiting an autopsy? Is her relationship with her boyfriend and that she was "never very secure" necessary? Should journalists list her boyfriend as a survivor? Should the obituary mention the daughter she gave up for adoption?

OBITUARY NOTICE: BARLOW
SPELLING ERRORS: The names Haselfe (not Haself), Kopperud (not Koperud) and Manuel (not Manual) are misspelled.
FACT ERRORS and NOTE: The addresses are incorrect: 3363 (not 3365) Andover Drive; 554 (not 544) Beloit Ave. (not Road.); 374 Douglas (not Douglass) Road; 4187 (not 1487) N. 14th St. (not just 14th St.). Should addresses be included?
ETHICAL ISSUES: Should a reporter write that a body was "donated for transplants, with remains to be cremated and scattered"? What should be mentioned about Barlow's being gay and his commitment ceremony with Bernaiche? Should journalists list Bernaiche among the survivors?

Chapter 12. Speeches and Meetings

Exercise 1. Evaluating Speech and Meeting Leads

1. Grade: A. The lead is clear and specific. It is also concise and emphasizes facts likely to interest readers.

2. Grade: D. The lead essentially restates the speaker's topic, something that may have been announced weeks or even months earlier. This lead should summarize the speaker's comments about crime and its impact upon families.

3. Grade: B. The lead clearly summarizes the council's action but might be even more specific. Why was the vote so close? Why did the council reject it?

4. Grade: D. This is a label lead. It reports only that a debate took place without summarizing or reporting its outcome. In addition, the lead contains a cliché. Most debates are "heated."

5. Grade: B. The lead begins with a clear summary of the speaker's remarks and limits the attribution to seven words. However, the lead uses an unfamiliar name. Because many readers would wonder who Sota is, the lead might use her title rather than her name. Or, it might present other details that would show she is a knowledgeable source.

6. Grade: B. The lead summarizes the meeting's outcome, and it emphasizes facts most likely to interest students. A stronger lead would include why the fees will increase.

7. Grade: C. This label lead identifies the speaker and his topic but fails to report what he said about the topic.

8. Grade: C. The lead should summarize the news: the comments those 20 people made about plans to license and regulate snowmobiles. Did they favor or oppose the plans? Why?

9. Grade: D. The lead focuses on government procedures and says nothing about how the commission's action might affect readers.

10. Grade: F. The story deserves an automatic "F" because it misspells the mayor's name: Datolli (not Datoli). Normally, the lead might receive a "C." It would receive a higher grade if it summarized the mayor's defense of the plan.

11. Grade: C. The lead starts well, with a clear, simple, startling summary of Madea's views. But it violates a simple rule: "Show, don't tell." Here, the author calls Madea's speech "fiery," but fails to present any specific details to support that conclusion. Thus, the attribution seems vague and exaggerated.

12. Grade: B. The lead summarizes the council's action but might be more specific. It might explain the reason for or significance of the decision.

13. Grade: F. The lead contains a grammatical error (The word "board" is singular and "their" plural). Thus, the lead should state, "...the board proceeded through its agenda." In addition, the lead emphasizes the fact that business flowed smoothly, which is unlikely to interest readers.

14. Grade: D. The lead contains a grammatical error (The word "commission" is singular, not plural). The lead should state, "The County Commission continued to struggle ... at its (not their) meeting Monday. It eventually denied a petition to build a new boat ramp on the lake." Also, the lead leaves the reader wondering what is the connection between the boat ramp and water quality and why the Commission struggled to reach a decision.

15. Grade: B. The lead is clear and concise and summarizes a topic likely to interest — and perhaps surprise — many readers. The lead is a bit long, but nicely presented in two sentences.

Exercise 3. Speech: The Police and the Press

ETHICAL ISSUE: The police chief tells of a college student who accidentally killed himself during autoerotic asphyxiation. Should the story include that? The police chief also describes a couple of murder cases. How much detail about the victims' deaths should the story include?

Exercise 6. Speech: Clinton's Memorial Address

FACTUAL ERROR: Pan Am Flight 103 crashed in Lockerbie, Scotland, Dec. 21, 1988, after a terrorist's bomb exploded on board. It was not shot down.
LOCALIZATION OPPORTUNITY: Students in Oklahoma and Oklahoma City can localize this story.

Exercise 7. County Commission Meeting

SPELLING ERRORS: The names DiCesari (not DiCesare), Grauman (not Graumann) and Chenn (not Chen) are misspelled.

Exercise 8. School Board Meeting

ETHICAL ISSUE: One of the parents, Claire Sawyer, objects to biology books that "never mention the theory of creationism." The city directory reveals that Sawyer is a minister at Christian Redeemer Church. During the meeting, Sawyer never mentioned her religious affiliation or position at the church. Should reporters mention it in their stories?
FACTUAL ERRORS: Hubbard's first name is Gary (not Greg) and Cross' first name is Ray (not Roy).
SPELLING ERRORS: The names Dawson (not Dawsun), Paynick (not Paynich), Eulon (not Euon) are misspelled.

Exercise 9. City Council Meeting

ETHICAL ISSUE: Should students clean up the speakers' quotations, eliminating their grammatical errors and the words "uh" and "you know," for example? Should students also avoid using the word "damn"?
SPELLING ERRORS: The names Levin (not Levine), Louis (not Luis), Rafelsin (not Rafelson), Gandolf (not Bandolf) and Guzmann (not Guzman) are misspelled. The name Belmonte (not Belmont) is spelled inconsistently.

Chapter 13. Specialized Types of Stories

Exercise 1. Brights

1. **SPELLING ERRORS**: The names Brookes (not Brooks) and Ruffenbach (not Ruffenboch) are misspelled.
   FACTUAL ERROR: Kasparov's address is 9103 (not 9301) Lake St.
2. **SPELLING ERROR**: The name Patti (not Patty) is misspelled.
   NOTE: Students who consult the city directory will discover that DeLoy is a doctor and that Patrick McFerren is the U.S. postmaster — details that they should include in the story.
3. **NOTE**: Snyder was charged with drunken driving, not drunk driven.
   SPELLING ERROR: The name Kocembra (not Kosembra) is misspelled once.
4. **SEXISM ISSUE**: Note the story's use of the word "firemen."
5. **SPELLING ERROR**: The name Saterwaitte (not Satterwaite) is misspelled.
7. **NOTE**: "Filly horse" is redundant.
   SPELLING ERROR: The name Forsythe (not Forsyth) is misspelled.

Exercise 2. Follow-up Stories

SPELLING ERRORS: The names Heslinn (not Heslin) and Kopperud (not Koperud) are misspelled. The name McGorwann (not McGorwan) is spelled inconsistently.

Exercise 3. Follow-up Stories

FACTUAL ERROR: Hubbard's first name is Gary (not Greg).

Exercise 4. Follow-up Stories

SPELLING ERRORS: The names Sarah (not Sara), Fredric (not Frederick), Cheesbro (not Cheeseboro) and Rudnike (not Rudnick) are misspelled.

Exercise 5. Roundups — Multiple Sources

ETHICAL ISSUES: Should reporters use the word "damn" while quoting the fire chief? Also, should reporters correct the sources' grammatical errors and polish their direct quotations, eliminating words such as "uh"?
SEXISM ISSUE: Should reporters repeat the word "firemen" while quoting Minh?
SPELLING ERROR: The names Stephen (not Steven) and Hilten (not Hilton) are misspelled.

Exercise 6. Roundups — Multiple Events

FACTUAL ERROR: The correct address is 1413 (not 1314) Griesi (not Griese) Drive.

SEXISM ISSUE: The story uses the words "firemen," "repairman" and "spokesman." In addition, the story refers to "Mr. and Mrs. Timothy Keel" and quotes Mrs. Keel, but never uses her first name — only her husband's.
SPELLING ERRORS: The names Keel (not Keele) and Suzanne (not Susan) are misspelled.
NOTE: Mistakenly, some students report the fires in the order in which they are presented. Students should begin with the most newsworthy fire (the third, which caused a death.)

Exercise 7. Sidebars

SEXISM ISSUE: The story uses the words "men" and "fireman."
SPELLING ERRORS: The names Petchski (not Petchsky) and Haserott (not Haserot) are misspelled.

Exercise 8. Sidebars

ETHICAL ISSUE: Should reporters quote DiCesari's profanities?
NOTE: The exercise uses the word "she" to refer to the governor. The correct pronoun will vary from state to state, depending on the sex of your governor.
SPELLING ERROR: The name DiCesari (not DiCesare) is misspelled.

Chapter 14. Feature Stories

Exercise 3. Information for Features

2.   **SPELLING ERROR:** The name Carigg (not Carig) is spelled inconsistently.
     NOTE: Al Giangelli's parents are divorced. Is this relevant?

3.   **SPELLING ERRORS:** The street Holcroft (not Holcrofte) is misspelled, and the name Ann (not Anne) is spelled inconsistenly.
     FACT ERROR: The address is 1978 (not 1987) Holcroft Ave.
     NOTE: Should you use the name of a teen-age girl who admits she worked as a prostitute? A reporter apparently promised to keep her name a secret.

Chapter 15. Public Affairs Reporting

Exercise 1. A Child's Heroism

ETHICAL ISSUE: If reporters identify the 6-year-old child, they will also identify her mother, who was raped. But is it fair to identify the suspect and not the victim?

Exercise 2. The Dahmer Tapes

ETHICAL ISSUE: Should reporters clean up the caller's direct quotations, correcting her grammar, for example?
LOCALIZATION OPPORTUNITY: Students in Milwaukee can localize this story.

Exercise 3. Sheriff's Department

1.　**FACTUAL ERRORS**: DaRoza's address is 410 University Ave., not Boulevard
　　SPELLING ERRORS: Keel's home is on Griesi (not Griese) Dr.; Adler's first name is Stuard (not Stuart).
　　NOTE: Adler is a minister.
　　SEXISM ISSUE: Students should not assume the reporting officer is a man; "S. Cullinan" stands for "Susan Cullinan," a sheriff's deputy.
2.　**SPELLING ERROR**: Terest (not Terese) is misspelled.
　　NOTE: Marci Hall is a municipal court judge.

Exercise 5. Police Department

1.　**SPELLING ERRORS**: Ann (not Anne) is mispelled; Caspinwall (not Caspenwall) is misspelled.
2.　**SEXISM ISSUE**: Students should not assume the supervising officer is a man; "T. Dow" stands for "Tammy Dow," a police sergeant.
　　FACT ERROR: Danny Jones lives on Darlington Avenue (not Arlington).

Exercise 6. Fire Department

1.　**SEXISM ISSUE**: The report refers to Mr. and Mrs. Michael Deacosti and does not use Peggy Deacosti's first name.
2.　**NOTE**: Roger Lo is a member of the city council.

Exercise 7. Dowdell Complaint

FACTUAL ERRORS: Hubbard's first name is Gary (not Greg), and Ferrell's first name is Melvin (not Marvin).

Exercise 8. Williams Guardianship

SPELLING ERROR: The name Jon (not John) is misspelled.

Exercise 10. School District Budget

NOTE: Students can quickly check some of the superintendent's statements about the budget by entering the figures in a spreadsheet program or by using a calculator. For instance, the superintendent says salaries and fringe benefits will not increase, but a comparison of the numbers shows that salaries for teachers will rise 8 percent, even though the number of teachers is increasing only 2.4 percent. The numbers also show that per pupil spending from the general fund is increasing by more than $260.

Chapter 16. Understanding and Using the Internet

Exercise 1.

NOTE: Different search engines and subject directories and keywords and connectors will produce different results.

NOTE: Results of reliable information and URLs may take more than one search.

NOTE: The homepages presented here are not comprehensive, but are examples of Web sites with helpful information or links to helpful information.

NOTE: ProfNet or one of the people finder Web sites listed in the chapter will identify experts to interview. Search results will include various popular press and research journal articles. Authors and experts within specialized institutions are good sources.

1. www.epa.gov, www.ase.org, www.aceee.org
   NOTE: Search results should include state departments of environmental quality and university professors who are experts on environmental policy.

2. www.realtimes.com, www.demographics.com, www.census.gov
   NOTE: Search results might include university professors of sociology.

3. www.highwaysafety.org, www.ncadd.com, www.comnet.org, www.madd.org, thomas.loc.gov, www.iii.org
   NOTE: Search results should include state departments of transportation.

4. www.intellihealth.com, bookman.com.au/vitamins, www.mayohealth.org, www.dietary-supplements.info.nih.gov, www2.nas.edu
   NOTE: Search results should include physicians who specialize in vitamins and nutrition supplements.

Chapter 17. Advanced Reporting

Exercise 1. Television's Effects on Children

NOTE: Students should explore the "other side" of this issue, researching facts from those who disagree with the American Psychological Association's position. This exercise would be a good opportunity to use the Internet to contact groups or organizations that have a different viewpoint.

Exercise 3. Juvenile Shoplifter

LOCALIZATION OPPORTUNITY: Students at Georgia State University and at the University of Richmond can localize this story.

Exercise 4. Rates of Crime

LOCALIZATION OPPORTUNITY: Students in the nation's 40 largest cities can localize this story.

Exercise 5. Update On Adult Illiteracy

LOCALIZATION OPPORTUNITY: Students in every state can localize this story.

Exercise 6. From the Office of the Governor

LOCALIZATION OPPORTUNITY: Students in every state can localize this story.

Exercise 7. Conducting an Informal Poll

NOTE: Instructors may choose either to have their students write their stories based only on their own interviews or to have them pool their information. If students pool their information, they may type up their raw notes and give them to the instructor, who photocopies them for the entire class. Pooling the information lets the students draw on a larger body of interviews when they write their stories. They are also able to see and compare the notes taken by different members of the class. The careful note takers may set a helpful example for those students who ignore important details.

Chapter 18. Writing for Broadcast

Exercise 1. Identifying Broadcast Style

1. This lead is conversational and the verb is in the present tense. A newspaper story would have the attribution following the claim and be in the past tense. A newspaper lead would also tell us when the fraud was found and give an exact title for the government official.

2. A newspaper lead would have more solid information than this one, which is in the present tense, has fewer facts and has a conversational style. The state is written out for broadcast copy.

3. The use of the present tense, the placement of the attribution before the claim, and the creative punctuation indicating to the announcer a pause following Maggie Williams' name all mark this as a broadcast lead.

4. Where this lead uses the present perfect tense and a title instead of a name, a newspaper lead might use the past tense, spell out FBI on first reference and include when the event happened.

5. This lead is in the present perfect tense and conversational. A newspaper lead would be past tense, include the specific day and name of the agency seeking extradition.

6. A newspaper would include the names of the prosecutors and the city official, whereas this lead is in the present tense, is conversational and appears to be an update.

7. The lead is in the present tense and is an update. The time is assumed to be today. A newspaper would give the specific part of south Louisiana covered by the flash-flood watch area.

8. This lead emphasizes the latest news and is in the present tense. A newspaper lead would emphasize the shooting and the death of the fellow officer.

9. This lead contains the phonetic spelling for a word with which the announcer may not be familiar and is in the present tense. A newspaper would have given the name of the U.N. representative.

10. This lead is in the present perfect tense. A newspaper lead would give the specific place in Arkansas and perhaps the name of the restaurant.

Exercise 2. Identifying Different Broadcast Leads

1. UMBRELLA: "Accidents" indicates the story is about more than one incident.
2. THROWAWAY: The story makes sense without the lead.
3. SOFT: The lead gives important, but general information. The hard facts are in the second sentence.
4. HARD: Meaningful information is communicated first. The information affects all Lear personnel and the companies that Lear supplies.
5. THROWAWAY: The lead is unnecessary. The story makes sense without the first sentence.
6. HARD: The important information, that people are dead, is in the first sentence.
7. UMBRELLA: "Several U-S industries" in the lead indicates the story will include more than just the agriculture ("asparagus") industry.
8. THROWAWAY: The story really begins with the second sentence.
9. SOFT: The lead summarizes the story by giving general information, and sets the tone for understanding the story.
10. SOFT: The lead gives general information. The second sentence depends on the first.

Exercise 3. Writing Broadcast Stories

NOTE: The correct spellings of some of the names in Exercise 3 can be found in the city directory (Appendix A).

NOTE: For all stories, students should add shorter lines together when estimating a story's timing.

NOTE: Add phonetic spelling when necessary.

NOTE: Some stories refer to adults by their first names. Several stories use "that" while referring to people and "who" while referring to inanimate objects. There are instances subject/verb/pronoun/disagreement.

2.   **SPELLING ERRORS:** The names Pinero (not Pinaro) and Datolli (not Datoli) are spelled inconsistently.

       NOTE: Should the story refer to Pinero as J.T. or as Jim Timmons, the name that appears in the city directory?

3.   **SPELLING ERRORS:** The names Holten (not Holton) and McCartney (not McCartey) are spelled inconsistently.

       FACTUAL ERROR: According to the city directory, Judge LeClair has no middle initial.

4.   **SPELLING ERROR:** The name Barlow (not Barlew) is spelled inconsistently.

Exercise 4. Writing Shorter Broadcast Stories

NOTE: The correct spellings of some of the names in Exercise 4 can be found in the city directory (Appendix A).

NOTE: For all stories, students should add shorter lines together when estimating a story's timing.

NOTE: Add phonetic spelling when necessary.

NOTE: Some stories refer to adults by their first names. Several stories use "that" while referring to people and "who" while referring to inanimate objects. There are instances subject/verb/pronoun/disagreement.

1.   **SPELLING ERROR:** The name Gianangeli (not Giangeli) is misspelled, and the name Clauch (not Claunch) is spelled inconsistently.

3.   **SPELLING ERRORS:** The names Rivera (not Riviera) and Fusner (not Fuzner) are spelled inconsistently, and the name Nicholls (not Nichols) is misspelled. Also, Belgard (not Belgarde) is misspelled.

       FACTUAL ERRORS: The address 1287 (not 1872) Belgard Ave. (not Av.) is incorrect. Maxwell (not Max) is listed in the city directory.

Exercise 5. Writing Broadcast Stories

NOTE: The correct spellings of some of the names in Exercise 5 can be found in the city directory (Appendix A).

NOTE: For all stories, students should add shorter lines together when estimating a story's timing.

NOTE: Add phonetic spelling when necessary.
NOTE: Some stories refer to adults by their first names.
Several stories use "that" while referring to people and "who" while referring to inanimate objects. In addition, there are instances subject/verb/pronoun/disagreement.

1. **SPELLING ERRORS:** The names Carvel (not Caravel) and Gary (not Gerrie) are misspelled, and Hubbard (not Hubard) is spelled inconsistently.
   NOTE: After the city directory was published, Carvel changed jobs, from a teacher at Colonial Elementary School to vice principle at Central High School.

3. **SPELLING ERRORS:** The names Sarah (not Sara) and Barry (not Bary) are misspelled.
   NOTE: Kopperud (not Howard) is the speaker of the last quote, recommending Howard for the Medal of Valor.

4. **SPELLING ERROR:** The name Minnie (not Minny) is misspelled.
   NOTE: This story uses the word "businessman" while describing a woman, Minnie Cosby.

5. **SPELLING ERRORS:** The name DiCesari (not DeCassari) is misspelled, and Lyn (Lynn) is spelled inconsistently.
   FACTUAL ERROR: The address 488 (not 489) Tulip Dr. is incorrect.
   NOTES: The story identifies one of the victims with her husband's name. The city directory notes that Tracy Aneja is a carpenter. Should students mention the "pools of blood"? Or, is that unnecessarily sensational, in poor taste and a cliché?

Chapter 19. The News Media and the PR Practitioner

Exercise 1. Editing a News Release

This release contains numerous style errors in time elements, addresses and dates.

Exercise 3. Writing News Releases

2.   This release contains laudatory adjectives in the descriptions of participants.

Exercise 4. Writing News Releases

2.   This release contains puffery that should be eliminated.

Exercise 5. Evaluating News Releases

1.   This is a story that is likely to interest many women. While the lead is longer than most editors like, it does take a newsworthy approach to the issue.
2.   This lead may deal with an issue of interest to a number of people in the audience—high school seniors planning on going to college and their parents—but it backs into the news. In addition, it could be a promotional piece for Morris College.
3.   The lead provides details on the problems facing the agricultural community, but the story is not a new one. The agricultural community has been struggling economically for several decades and unless the study at the university reveals something new, editors probably would not use this story.
4.   The details in the lead are likely to interest, even shock, some audience members. But they are not new. The second paragraph describes a local event to be held Friday.
5.   The lead is too vague and too general and uses too many sentences to get to the point. It has low audience interest—affects only those who use electronic keys. This is obviously pushing a company and its product.
6.   Cannot use. Very low news value. The release is written more for a specialized market—the magazine and its industry. Also, magazines don't announce, people do.
7.   No news value. This is not the type of story that news organizations typically publish. Editors rarely promote commercial products and services. Rather, they would expect the store to buy an advertisement to promote the event.
8.   Moderate news value only if the gauges are widely used in the area. The release, however, cannot be used as written: The company and product are mentioned first, the injuries last. Most audience members would not read the verbiage to get to the news. Problems with AP style.
9.   Because the story would interest few audience members, most editors would skip it. If they did use the release, they might summarize it in a single paragraph, perhaps as part of a "promotions' or "news briefs" section.
10.   Many Americans suffer from arthritis, and this story might interest them. The story also might interest other people who fear that they may someday develop arthritis. Still, the story says nothing new. The problem has existed for some time and lacks a new angle.

Exercise 6. Eliminating Puffery

1. The entry deadline is March 16.
2. The company's president has hired older, disabled and homeless workers.
3. The Lake Street Players will stage the British farce "Run For Your Wife!" from May 25 to 27 and from May 31 to June 2, with each performance starting at 8 p.m.
4. The governor today announced the selection of 12 people who will serve on a search committee for a new chancellor for the state's university system.
5. Director Chris Allen will introduce a new musical comedy, "Love, Love, Love," at 7 p.m. Friday and Saturday and at 2 p.m. Sunday. The comedy is being staged at the Center for Arts and tickets cost $9.50.
6. While serving as head of the Chamber of Commerce in Houston, Johnson increased its membership 41 percent. Johnson will begin work as president of the chamber here next week and hopes to achieve the same type of rapid growth.
7. The cast includes Hans Gregory Ashbaker as Rodolfo and Elizabeth Holleque as Mimi. Holleque, a soprano, won the Metropolitan Opera National Council Auditions in 1983, and appeared here last season as Marguerite in "Faust."
8. Custom builders will open 18 models in the new Torey Pines subdivision at noon Sunday. The lots are in a pine forest and start at one-half acre, with prices for the homes beginning at $300,000.

Exercise 7. Rewriting News Releases

2. **SPELLING ERROR:** The name Ann Capiello (not Anne Marie Capielli) is misspelled.
3. This release is filled with military jargon that needs to be simplified.

Exercise 8. Rewriting News Releases

SPELLING ERROR: The name Matros (not Matroes) is misspelled.

Chapter 20: Communications Law

Exercise 1. Libel

1.   **DANGEROUS:** The sentences imply Andrews is guilty of assault on the police officers, even though he has not been convicted and his version of the incident has not been heard. Because it appears to be based on unofficial statements by the officers, it is not protected by qualified privilege.

2.   **SAFE:** So long as their accounts are fair and accurate, newswriters are immune from libel suits while reporting official government proceedings such as trials.

3.   **SAFE:** Note the story's careful wording. It never says that Kasandra is guilty, only that she has been <u>charged</u> with the crime.

4.   **SAFE:** The story cannot libel anyone because it never identifies a specific individual.

5.   **DANGEROUS:** The story is clearly libelous because it declares that White was drunk. Only official government proceedings, not the statements made by a police officer, are protected by "privilege."
     SPELLING ERROR: The name Katherine (not Catherine) is misspelled.

6.   **SAFE:** Americans are free to criticize government agencies and officials. A large city such as Cleveland employs thousands of people, and this story does not identify any of them by name.

7.   **SAFE:** Presidents are public figures, and Americans are free to express their opinions of them, even opinions harshly critical of them.

8.   **SAFE:** The doctrine of fair comment protects journalists who criticize, even harshly, products offered to the public.

9.   **DANGEROUS:** The story is clearly libelous. Before any determination by a court, it convicts Guitterman, calling him "the biggest drug dealer in the city." The story is also unfair to Guitterman. If, months later, a jury finds Guitterman innocent, his reputation will have been ruined.
     SPELLING ERROR: The name Guitterman (not Guiterman) is misspelled.

10. **DANGEROUS:** The story reports a lawsuit's claim that Tifton struck a police officer. Then, going beyond the lawsuit, the story seems to call Tifton a criminal.
     NOTE: Tifton is a captain in your city's fire department, a detail that would normally be included in the story.

11. **DANGEROUS:** The janitor has not been charged with a crime. Yet people who read this story may know the janitor's identity, even though his name is not used, and conclude that he is guilty of molesting several boys.

Exercise 2. Libel

The accusations Davis made against Fong probably are defamatory. Saying that Fong has used union funds to hire prostitutes is clearly defamatory. Hiring prostitutes is a crime, and accusations of criminal conduct are libelous. Misuse of union funds may be a felony, and even though hiring a prostitute may be only a misdemeanor, the accusation could be enough to discourage some people from association with Fong or doing business with him. It certainly could make people think less of him. The accusation that he broke his promise to union members to keep them informed about the labor negotiations also may be defamatory. It calls into question Fong's competence and trustworthiness in performing his job.

The news that Fong had been convicted of automobile theft and spent time in the state penitentiary is also defamatory. Most people are suspicious of ex-convicts and avoid having anything to do with them.

The comment by Paula Williams is crude but probably not defamatory. Calling Fong an S.O.B. and a bastard is not the kind of thing that can be proved true or false; therefore, it cannot be the basis for a libel suit. The statement that Fong is trying to "extort a fortune" from the city probably is not defamatory either. Extortion is a crime, but taken in context, Williams' remark is not an accusation of criminal conduct. It is merely a colorful description of Fong's bargaining technique.

On these facts, Fong probably would be able to prove most of the other elements of a libel suit. The story was published and one can assume that Fong was clearly identified in the story, since it was a profile of Fong. The fact that the union's investigation concluded that Fong had not misused union money would be evidence that the most serious of the defamatory statements was false. The part of the story that described his prison record also was false to the extent that it incorrectly said he had spent five years in prison. There is no evidence, however, that the allegation he kept union members in the dark about the negotiations is false.

The common-law defenses will provide little help for the Beacon Daily Light. The story seems to be clearly false in alleging that Fong used union funds to hire prostitutes. That part of the story is not based on official records or proceedings, so the newspaper cannot claim qualified privilege. Nor is the allegation an opinion; it clearly alleges specific facts. The report of Fong's prison term may be substantially true, since the sting of the defamatory statement — that he served time for automobile theft — is true.

A crucial issue for the Beacon Daily Light is whether Fong is a public figure. He is not a public official; he works for the union, not the city. But as the union's chief negotiator, he occupies a leadership position on a issue of clear public importance: the contract negotiations between the city and its workers. The contentious nature of the negotiations suggests that they have become a public controversy, and Fong is at the center of it. Therefore, he probably is a public figure for the purpose of commenting on his role in the labor talks. He must prove actual malice to recover damages, meaning he must show that Jackson and others at the newspaper knew the story was false or had a high degree of awareness of its probable falsity.

The error in reporting the length of time Fong served in prison probably was not made with actual malice. The error arose from Jackson's failure to read the entire record. She was negligent, but nothing suggests she had a high degree of awareness of the story's falsity.

There is no evidence that Jackson knew the story was false, but there is evidence that she acted recklessly in publishing the allegations from Davis. Davis told her that he suspected Fong had been using union money to hire prostitutes, and presumably Jackson quoted Davis correctly. But Davis's grudge against Fong and his alcoholism make him an unreliable source. Also, Davis told Jackson to check with the union's bookkeeper to confirm the story. She never did. If she had, she might have learned before publication what the union learned only later: that union funds were not misused. Relying entirely on an untrustworthy source is evidence of actual malice. So is failing to check a source who possesses evidence that can prove or disprove an allegation. The Supreme Court has said juries may presume from such conduct that the publisher strongly suspected the falsity of the story and purposefully failed to check it out. Because Fong probably can prove actual malice, he will not have to prove actual injury, although his wife's decision to divorce him suggests he would be able to prove loss of reputation.

In short, Fong has a chance of winning a libel suit over the publication of the accusation that he used union money to hire prostitutes, even though he is a public figure and must prove actual malice. He would have little chance of recovering damages for any of the other statements published in Jackson's story.

ETHICAL ISSUES: Should a reporter include Williams' profanity? The reporter and the newspaper probably cannot be sued for publishing the derogatory statements Williams made during a public meeting of the city council, but do reporters and news organizations have an ethical obligation to refrain from using such statements? Should the reporter have interviewed Fong before publishing this story? What should the reporter do if Fong refused to be interviewed?

Exercise 3. Libel

The Nightly News has managed to defame Starr, Vernon and Grady in its report by accusing them of engaging in a conspiracy to violate federal law. The law prohibits sending arms and supplies to the Costa Grande rebels, but the story directly accuses Starr of doing just that. It also says Vernon knowingly financed this illegal operation and Grady tried to obstruct a federal investigation of their activities. All of this is criminal conduct and, therefore, defamatory on its face. The story was published and all were identified. Also, chances are good all of them would be able to show their reputations have been impaired and that they have suffered mental anguish.

Some parts of the story seem to have a sound factual basis; others do not. The evidence seems fairly strong that Starr has participated in the illegal arms trade. The network has information from people actually involved in the trade. These are mostly convicted felons, people who are inherently untrustworthy, but their allegations are supported by evidence from congressional staff members who have seen classified reports on Starr's dealings. The fact that Starr denies the charges does not make them false.

The allegation that Vernon put up millions of dollars for this illegal enterprise also has plenty of support. The Nightly News reporters drew information from people who helped managed the Vernon family's fortune, and presumably they would have first-hand knowledge of how the money was spent. The report did err in calculating the amount of money Vernon had given to support the Costa Grande rebels. Apparently she gave $2.3 million, rather than $3 million. The story remains substantially true, in spite of that error.

The part of the story about Grady's efforts to obstruct a federal investigation of the illegal arms trade has less evidence. The story relied entirely on the word of one State Department worker who wants Grady's job.

Whether Starr, Vernon and Grady must prove actual malice will have a major impact on the case. Starr most likely is a public figure and Grady is a public official, both of whom must prove actual malice. Vernon's status is unclear. The problem of the Costa Grande rebels has been a major one in Congress and has been in the news for some time. Starr has voluntarily played an important role in trying to influence public opinion about the issue by his television appearances and writings. He would seem to fit the definition of a limited-purpose public figure. Grady is the government official with responsibility for formulating and carrying out U.S. policy in Central America. This would satisfy the criteria for being a public official.

Vernon, however, is in a gray area. She has used her money to advance the cause of the Costa Grande rebels and to shape public opinion about the issue. But she, herself, has remained silent. Her wealth alone would make her neither a general-purpose public figure nor a limited-purpose public figure. Her actions indicate that she has tried to remain a private person. Therefore, she probably is not a public figure and does not have to prove actual malice.

Starr probably will not be able to win his suit. There is no indication that the parts of story about him are false, and even if he were to produce such evidence, nothing suggests that any Nightly News reporter or producer doubted the truth of the story at the time it was broadcast. The fact the network's reporters ignored the sources Starr recommended is not evidence of actual malice. They apparently made a good-faith determination that those sources had no direct knowledge of the issue.

Vernon has little more chance of success than Starr, even though she must prove only negligence. The network probably was negligent in reporting that she had contributed $3 million rather than $2.3 million to Starr's organization. In spite of that negligence, however, the story remains substantially true. Unless Vernon can produce more evidence of falsity, she will lose.

Grady, however, has a good chance of recovering damages. The network's reporters relied entirely on a source whose credibility is questionable because of the grudge he holds against Grady. Furthermore, the source gave an improbable explanation of how he learned about Grady's cover-up efforts: a telephone glitch that conveniently allow him to overhear high officials. The reporters could have checked with the FBI to find out whether Grady had tried to interfere with the bureau's work, but they did not. The jury may decide that the reporters' failure to check was evidence that they were aware of the story's probable falsity and sought to avoid evidence that would prove it false.

ETHICAL ISSUE: At least some of the information for this story comes from convicted felons. Should a news organization ever use such information? If so when and with what precautions?

Exercise 4. Privacy

Lynd has a good chance of winning her lawsuit on grounds of appropriation, false light and intrusion. She also may be able to recover damages for publicity to private facts.

Appropriation is the use of another's name or likeness for one's benefit. The Intelligencer used Lynd's name in advertisements promoting its story about her and the rape accusation. When news organizations use in advertisements the names or likenesses of the people on whom they report, it normally is not appropriation unless the advertisements suggest that the person has endorsed the publication. The Intelligencer's ads suggest that Lynd has endorsed the tabloid, not only by talking to its reporters — which she did not do — but by depending on it to deliver the truth.

Any intrusion on another person's solitude or seclusion that would be highly offensive to a reasonable person may be actionable. The Intelligencer's photographers used powerful telephoto lenses to get photographs of Lynd in her backyard, which is surrounded by a privacy fence. Reasonable people who put up privacy fences do not expect to be photographed in their yards; therefore, the conduct of the photographers amounts to intrusion, even though they did not physically enter Lynd's property. Normally, photographing people in public places is not intrusion, but in this case, the Intelligencer's photographers aggressively followed Lynd to the point that they caused an accident on the freeway. This, too, may be intrusion.

False light is falsely portraying a person in a highly offensive manner and doing so with the knowledge that it was false or with reckless disregard for whether it was false. The Intelligencer falsely reported that Lynd consulted an astrologer about her business decisions. Although saying that a person consults an astrologer is not defamatory — many people do so — a successful business person may be highly offended to have one's success falsely attributed to a reliance on astrology. The only source for the story that Lynd relied on an astrologer came from an old friend who had not seen her for many years, a source who probably does not possess reliable information. A more reliable source is the astrologer, and he denies that Lynd is one of his clients. The fact that the Intelligencer's editors and reporters relied on a poor source and ignored a credible one, together with the editor's remark that the tabloid had a chance for revenge against Lynd, all suggest that the journalists published the story with knowledge that it was false or with reckless disregard for the truth.

The most difficult part of the lawsuit for Lynd will be proving that the Intelligencer gave publicity to private facts. This requires proving that the publisher revealed private facts, that a reasonable person would find such disclosures highly offensive, and that the publication served no legitimate public interest. Several of the facts the Intelligencer reported may not have been widely known, but they were on the public record. News organizations cannot be sued to publishing information obtained from public sources. All of the information obtained from court records about her arrests for speeding and drunken driving, the fact that her husband divorced her on grounds of infidelity, and information about her business dealings comes from public records and cannot be the basis for a lawsuit.

Much of the information the Intelligencer obtained from interviews is private, but even some of this information may be protected from a lawsuit. Reports that she had an irrational fear of food preservatives, chewed her fingernails and always slept in the nude may be mildly embarrassing, but not highly offensive. The same is true of reports of that she had been a "party girl" in high school, was a poor student and frequently was in trouble. The passage of time, however, may entitle Lynd to somewhat greater protection on these matters. If so, there may be some question about how great a public interest there is in her high school career. The public interest may extend beyond the issue that brought a person into the news and include other newsworthy aspects of that person's life. The fact that Lynd apparently has become a successful model, movie star and business person in spite of a troubled high school career may be of legitimate public interest.

One fact that seems to satisfy all the criteria for a publicity to private facts suit is the report that she contracted a venereal disease from her lover and transmitted it to her husband. The fact that she was divorced and that the grounds were infidelity are public record. The matter of the venereal disease was not, however. Intelligencer reporters learned that from interviewing the former husband. Even though he disclosed the information voluntarily, the Intelligencer still may be invading Lynd's privacy by publishing it. Disclosing that a person has had a venereal disease would be highly offensive to a reasonable person, given the sensitivity most people have about sexual matters. The information would seem to serve no legitimate public interest other than to titillate readers. Therefore, she probably can recover damages for this publication.

> **ETHICAL ISSUE:** Most state laws neither conceal the names of rape victims nor forbid their publication. Nevertheless, most news organizations refrain from publishing such names. Should the Weekly Intelligencer have refrained from identifying Jasmine Lynd as a rape victim?

Chapter 21: Ethics

Exercise 2. Stories That Raise Ethical Issues

NOTE: Students should think about the objective of the story and the reason for publishing it when choosing facts to include. Do these facts help achieve the objective of the story? When considering ethical problems, students should ask, "Who will be hurt, and how many?" and "Who will be helped, and how many?"

1. NURSING HOME EMPLOYEES
ETHICAL ISSUES:
A. Some people consider the term "ex con" derogatory. Should students use it in their stories?
B. Should students identify the nursing home that employs two former prostitutes?
C. Should students identify a man convicted of molesting children in 1981, and who has not been in any trouble since his release from prison in 1993?
D. Should students mention two allegations impossible to verify: allegations that some nursing homes restrained or sedated residents?
E. The story calls Rosolowski a "spokesman."

2. TEEN GANG
SPELLING ERRORS: The names Dolmovich (not Dolomovich), Grauman (not Graumann) and Kopperud (not Kopperuddd) are spelled inconsistently, and Alice (not Alyce) is spelled incorrectly.
ETHICAL ISSUES:
A. Is the students' race relevant? Should it be reported?
B. Should news stories identify both the suspects and their parents?
C. Should the story say a suspect's mother is divorced and on welfare and the suspect's father has disappeared?
D. Is it important to include that Gandolf is the widow of a City Council member and that Grauman is a local minister?

3. BOY'S MURDER
SPELLING ERRORS: The names Clauch (not Claunch) and Biagi (not Biaggi) are misspelled.
FACT ERROR: The address is 2418 (not 2481) Seasons Court.
ETHICAL ISSUES:
A. Should students report the allegations of torture?
B. Should students report the victim's criminal record? Is it relevant, or is it unnecessarily damaging to the victim's reputation?
C. Should students report unproven allegations that the victim: 1) belonged to a gang and 2) "was dealing drugs"?
D. Note the poor grammar and poor vocabulary used in this story. Should it be corrected?

SECTION VIII

TESTS

For your convenience, the following tests may be cut from this manual and duplicated. Or you can construct your own quizzes covering several chapters by selecting and duplicating some of the questions from each chapter. The answers for the true-and-false questions follow the quizzes.

Style Quiz

Name:_____   Date:_____

INSTRUCTIONS: Use the proper copy-editing symbols to correct all the mechanical, spelling and stylistic errors in the following sentences. The names in the sentences are spelled correctly.

1. The clubs advisor, Reverend Sue Holt of Little Rock Arkansas spent two thousand dollars during her vacation in the East last Summer.

2. Irregardless of the cost, James Hazard Sr., a realtor in East Lansing michigan agreed to help the Vice-President win 60% of the delegates.

3. On Tuesday August 13 the thirty two year old woman, a Journalism Professor in Ore. donated 5000 dollars to the democratic party.

4. 23 persons, all employes of the Federal Government, will attend the program, scheduled for 7:00 pm Tuesday December 18 in Oshkosh, Wisc.

5. His number one candidate, Dist. Atty. Lisa Diaz of 87 North Roosevelt Dr. complained that only four percent of the F.B.I. agents are women.

6. Both "Time Magazine" and "The Chicago Tribune" reported that James R Bughi, a presidential candidate, spent $42,000,000 dollars last fall.

7. 37 students in the philosophy class taught by Prof. Carlos Alicea finished the book entitled "American Outrage" before December 12.

8. The girl, age 19, recieved a broken arm when her ford van overturned 3 times while traveling 80 mph on interstate 80 near Des Moines, Ia.

9. Doctor Maria Chavez, the Mayor of San Antonio Texas said the vice-president and first lady will speak to the Sophomores next Winter.

10. During the 1980s, Lynita Wong, now a sgt. in the US army, studied english, history, french, and sociology at 3 colleges in the south.

Style Quiz

Name:_____   Date:_____

INSTRUCTIONS: Use the proper copy-editing symbols to correct all the mechanical, spelling and stylistic errors in the following sentences. The names in the sentences are spelled correctly.

1. During the 1980s, a nine year old girl in Ruston Louisiana won a trophy, 5000 dollars, and a trip to the United States Capital Bldg.

2. Thomas Shriver Junior an employe of the Roess Company in Fairbanks Alaska has a Ph.D. in economics and will be here Mon, Tues., & Wed.

3. Prof. Rebecca Malone of Forty-two Fifth Avenue works in the History Department and shares an office in Rm. 247 of the Humanities Bldg.

4. Afterwards, 7 persons, all United States citizens, testified that the US navy payed the Westinghouse Corporation $14,200,000 dollars.

5. "The Washington Post" reported Tue. that the suspect is White, in her 30's, about 5 ft., 2 inches tall, and weighs about one hundred pds.

6. Only one media reported that the President of the National Rifle Assn. met with sixteen members of the US Congress on August 14, 1987.

7. During the 1960's, a committee of the United States Congress estimated that the program would cost $7 to $8.4 billion dollars.

8. The boy, age 7, had 42 cents and said his mother, the Mayor, will attend the P.T.A. meeting Nov. 28 if the temperature remains above 0.

9. It was an unusual phenomena. During the twentieth century, the odds were 9 to 1 that 80% of the Mayors would be reelected to a 2nd term.

10. Moving backwards, the 14 yr old babysitter in Martin Tn. said goodbye, then picked up the bible and ran towards her home on Roe St.

Vocabulary Quiz

Name:_____   Date:_____

INSTRUCTIONS: Some words in the following sentences have been placed in parentheses: words that often cause confusion because they look or sound like other words. Decide which of the words is correct here and circle it. Cross off the other words. Also correct the sentences' possessives.

1. The prison (trustee/trusty) said it is (to/too) tiring and he fears (loosing/losing) his (role/roll) in the play (entitled/titled) "Sin."

2. After the (naval/navel) forces (ravaged/ravished) the city, the ships sailed (to/too) a (cite/sight/site) (farther/further) north.

3. A (censor/censure) (convinced/persuaded) the correspondent that her story was (liable/libel) to (affect/effect) the armys (moral/morale).

4. The schools (principal/principle) said bad (weather/whether) may (affect/effect) the students plans to build a nature (trail/trial).

5. Her (fiancé/fiancee) has (fewer/less) than a dozen of the (statues/statutes) but is (confidant/confident) that he can buy more.

6. Hundreds of the schools (alumna/alumni/alumnus) (adviced/advised) (its/it's) president to (altar/alter) (their/there/they're) seating.

7. The (consul/council/counsel) is (composed/comprised) of seven (people/persons) who (than/then) fired the city (marshal/marshall).

8. The data (are/is) confusing, and he (complemented/complimented) the (aides/aids) (incite/insight) but (adviced/advised) them to make some (miner/minor) changes in (their/there/they're) plans.

9. The (alumna/alumni/alumnus), a 50-year-old (blond/blonde) who (emigrated/immigrated) from Norway, lives in the state (capital/ capitol) and said she is trying to (adapt/adept/adopt) two children.

Vocabulary Quiz

Name:_____   Date:_____

INSTRUCTIONS: Some words in the following sentences have been placed in parentheses: words that often cause confusion because they look or sound like other words. Decide which of the words is correct here and circle it. Cross off the other words. Also correct the sentences' possessives.

1. He said a large (bloc/block) of voters wants to (canvas/canvass) the city (to/too) determine whether voters like the (ordinance/ordnance).

2. (To/too) (ensure/insure) (their/there/they're) success, he wants to move (foreward/forward) and (altar/alter) the parade route.

3. A federal (marshal/marshall) seized (above/more than/over) 200 of the dollar bills (that/which) the counterfeiters had (altared/altered).

4. He (cited/sighted/sited) a book (entitled/titled) "Now," and said that more (than/then) 100,000 (people/persons) purchased copies.

5. A dozen (media/medium) (are/is) investigating charges that students (hanged/hung) the coach in effigy, then (incited/insighted) the riot.

6. He was struck by the (forth/fourth) (foul/fowl) ball and remained (conscience/conscious) but said he wanted (to/too) (lay/lie) down.

7. He tried to (pedal/peddle) the bike (foreword/forward) on the path but could not (because/since) the (angel/angle) was (to/too) sharp.

8. The woman, a (blond/blonde), started the (pole/poll) and, (to/too) (ensure/insure) (its/it's) success, mailed 740 (envelopes/envelops).

9. The answer was (elusive/illusive), but the committee was (composed/comprised) of 12 students (adapt/adept/adopt) at determining (who's/whose) error caused the bitter (decent/descent/dissent).

107

Attribution Quiz

Name:_____   Date:_____

INSTRUCTIONS: Make any changes necessary to improve the attribution in the following sentences and paragraphs, and correct matters of style

1.   "No comment." "That's none of your business." said he.

2.   She said: "always laugh at yourself first — before others do".

3.   She said people who seek advice. "Are looking for an accomplice".

4.   "Only through self-discipline" claimed he "Can you achieve freedom."

5.   "Mealtime." she said. "Is when my kids sit down to continue eating."

6.   "If you rest you rust," actress Helen Hayes responded on her 90th birthday when asked by a

        reporter whether she would retire.

7.   "People think we make $3 million or $5 million a year." They don't realize that most athletes

        make only $500,000 the ballplayer said.

8.   If you knew how meat was made, you'd probably "lose your lunch." she said. "I know." she

        continued. "That's why I became a vegetarian." "It's a dirty, bloody, filthy process." she

        concluded.

9.   "My dad told me, "Americans suffer under the illusion that everything can be cured by passing a

        new law." My dad was right, of course Most things can't be solved by a new law." said Karpov.

10.   "Your food stamps will be stopped effective March 1 because we received notice that you passed

        away." "May God bless you." said a letter the county's Department of Social Services sent to a

        dead person. The letter then continued by adding that "You may reapply if there is a change in

        your circumstances."

Spelling Quiz

Name:_____   Date:_____

INSTRUCTIONS: These are 60 of the words that college students frequently misspell. Some of the words are spelled correctly, but many others are misspelled. Use the proper copy-editing symbols to correct all the misspelled words. If several letters need to be corrected in a single word, rewrite the entire word.

1.	accomodate	21.	govermental	41.	pryed
2.	advertizing	22.	gubernatorial	42.	recieve
3.	a lot	23.	hemorrhage	43.	reelect
4.	attendents	24.	labeled	44.	reguardless
5.	babysit	25.	lieutenant	45.	respondent
6.	backwards	26.	lightening	46.	saleries
7.	becomming	27.	likable	47.	sargeant
8.	benefit	28.	likelyhood	48.	schedule
9.	cemetery	29.	liscense	49.	sentance
10.	criticised	30.	maintnance	50.	seperate
11.	develope	31.	marijuana	51.	severly
12.	dieing	32.	mispell	52.	sheriff
13.	disastous	33.	mosquitos	53.	sophmore
14.	distroyed	34.	occured	54.	summerize
15.	drunkenness	35.	opperturnity	55.	surgery
16.	elite	36.	payed	56.	surprizing
17.	existence	37.	picknicing	57.	teenager
18.	favortism	38.	popular	58.	tenative
19.	foreigner	39.	practise	59.	wreckless
20.	fourty	40.	priviledge	60.	written

109

Spelling Quiz

Name:_____   Date:_____

INSTRUCTIONS: These are 60 of the words that college students frequently misspell. Some of the words are spelled correctly, but many others are misspelled. Use the proper copy-editing symbols to correct all the misspelled words. If several letters need to be corrected in a single word, rewrite the entire word.

1. accidentally	21. explaination	41. personel
2. adviser	22. goodbye	42. prepairing
3. ambulance	23. grammer	43. questionaire
4. ammendment	24. gray	44. quizes
5. amount	25. harrass	45. realised
6. apparently	26. heros	46. restaurant
7. arguement	27. imitate	47. singuler
8. athletics	28. indorsed	48. sking
9. axe	29. inocculate	49. souvenir
10. burglers	30. irate	50. sucessfull
11. circuit	31. judgement	51. sueing
12. contraversial	32. kindergarden	52. temperture
13. controled	33. magazines	53. thier
14. credibility	34. mathmatics	54. truely
15. cryed	35. media (plural)	55. trys
16. desparately	36. necessary	56. untill
17. deviding	37. nickles	57. vaccinate
18. dilema	38. ninety	58. vicious
19. embarass	39. occasionally	59. victum
20. equipted	40. occurence	60. Wedesday

110

Chapter 1. The Basics: Format and AP Style

True/False Questions

Name:_____

1._____   A slugline is another name for a headline.

2._____   Journalists begin each story about one-third of the way down the first page.

3._____   Reporters no longer use copy-editing symbols because the computer checks everything for them.

4._____   The beginning of a paragraph is indented three spaces.

5._____   Beginning journalists should be able to type at least 30 words per minute.

6._____   Whenever journalists make a mistake, such as a misspelling, they retype the story.

7._____   The Latin word "stet" means a proper name has been checked.

8._____   To indicate that a lower-case letter should be capitalized, journalists draw three lines under the letter.

9._____   Journalists spell out most numbers below 10.

10._____   It does not matter if a correction goes above or below the line to be corrected.

11._____   A small amount of sloppiness is tolerated in newsrooms and classrooms.

12._____   The Associated Press Stylebook and Libel Manual encourages consistency.

13._____   A factual error may seriously harm people mentioned in the story.

14._____   Most newspapers underline words for emphasis.

15._____   A factual error will damage a news organization's reputation.

Chapter 2. Grammar and Spelling

True/False Questions

Name:_____

1._____   Good reporters need only a nose for news.

2._____   Journalists must understand the basics of good grammar.

3._____   Most simple sentences have a subject, a verb and a direct object.

4._____   Verbs that have direct objects are called intransitive verbs.

5._____   Some exceptions to the rules allow using plural nouns with singular verbs.

6._____   Sentences that use the subject-verb-direct object order are active voice sentences.

7._____   Too many pronouns can lead to ambiguity.

8._____   "It's" reflects possession.

9._____   Singular and plural nouns ending in "s" need just an apostrophe to form a possessive.

10._____   "To whom did you give the ball?" is grammatically correct.

11._____   Modifiers qualify some other word or phrase.

12._____   "The car took a left turn" is grammatically correct.

13._____   Pronouns should agree with their antecedents.

14._____   "A," "an" and "the" are personifications.

15._____   Readers and viewers' biggest complaint about media is accuracy.

Chapter 3. Newswriting Style

True/False Questions

Name:_____

1._____   Researchers have been unable to find any correlation between a story's readability and sentence length.

2._____   The typical newspaper story is written at the educational level of a sixth grader.

3._____   Sentences that use the normal word order — subject, verb, direct object — tend to be both more concise and more readable.

4._____   Today's editors have abandoned the concept of objectivity.

5._____   Reporters who fail to properly attribute their sources' opinions will seem to be presenting their own opinions.

6._____   Reporters are expected to avoid occupational terms that exclude women: terms such as "fireman," "mailman" and "policeman."

7._____   Reporters are expected to observe and report the fact that a person is a "woman doctor" or "female general," for example.

8._____   Reporters are also expected to describe the physical characteristics of women in the news: their hair, dress, voice and figure, for example.

9._____   The simple words and sentences that people use while speaking to friends are inappropriate in news stories.

10._____   Most of the newspapers examined by a committee of the American Society of Newspaper Editors were written at the 12th grade level or higher.

11._____   Good writers such as Ernie Pyle and Edna Buchanan avoid three- and four-word sentences.

12._____   A good newswriter will first introduce a topic, then present some specific information about it.

13._____   Editors encourage some repetition: repeating key facts for emphasis.

14._____   Newswriters should mention the marital status of women in the news: whether they are single, married or divorced.

15._____   Reporters use a central point in a story to tell readers what they will learn from reading the entire story.

Chapter 4. The Language of News

True/False Questions

Name:_____

1._____   A car can collide with a building.

2._____   The use of active verbs makes sentences more concise as well as more interesting.

3._____   Editors encourage use of the verbs "is," "are," "was" and "were."

4._____   Reporters avoid clichés because they require too much originality, thought and time.

5._____   Newspaper editors encourage the use of words such as "cop," "authored" and "passed away."

6._____   The term "journalese" identifies clichés that are commonly associated with news writing.

7._____   After a robbery and murder, it would be accurate to report that the gunman "produced" a weapon and "executed" a clerk.

8._____   News writers avoid adverbs and adjectives because they comment on the facts of a story instead of just reporting the facts.

9._____   Editors encourage the use of slang because it is familiar and easy to understand.

10._____   Reporters are expected to recognize and avoid the jargon used by sources such as doctors, lawyers and business people.

11._____   Reporters use euphemisms when they want to say something as bluntly as possible.

12._____   Clauses introduced by "that" are essential to the meaning of a sentence; those introduced by "which" add helpful, but not necessary, information.

13._____   News writers may use "that" and "which" to introduce clauses that refer to people or animals with names.

14._____   Good reporters avoid echoes, gush, parenthetical matter, platitudes and first-person references in their stories.

15._____   Americans are more likely to use platitudes than euphemisms while talking about death and other unpleasant topics.

Chapter 5. Selecting and Reporting the News

True/False Questions

Name:_____

1._____ Journalists' selection of news is subjective, not scientific.

2._____ Al Neuharth complains that, like other newspapers, USA Today practices a "Journalism of Despair."

3._____ Definitions of news vary from one medium to another.

4._____ Newspapers' policies are set by their editors and publishers, not reporters.

5._____ When a federal judge ruled that lyrics sung by the rap group 2 Live Crew were obscene, most newspapers published the lyrics so readers could judge the material for themselves.

6._____ Young adults are newspapers' most avid readers.

7._____ An experiment conducted in Miami demonstrated that newspapers can de-emphasize violence and still give their readers an accurate and complete picture of the world.

8._____ While selecting the news, editors try to provide an accurate portrayal of the life of normal people during a typical day in a their community.

9._____ As a matter of policy, news organizations are reluctant to report rumors.

10._____ It does not seem to matter whether a story is long or short. No more than about half the readers who start any story will finish it.

11._____ The goal of public journalism, its proponents say, is to encourage more people to participate in public life.

12._____ The prominence of a person involved in an event has no impact on the event's newsworthiness.

13._____ Newspapers can use a trade name such as "Kleenex" to describe similar products manufactured by different companies.

Chapter 6. Basic News Leads

True/False Questions

Name:_____

1._____ Every lead should answer six questions: Who? How? Where? Why? When? and What?

2._____ A good lead often continues for four or five typed lines.

3._____ Editors encourage "blind leads" but not "label leads."

4._____ Reporters should place the explanation after, not before, a list in their lead.

5._____ Leads must follow all the normal rules for punctuation, grammar, word usage and verb tenses.

6._____ Every lead must contain only one sentence.

7._____ Four of the best verbs for leads are "is," "are" "was" and "were."

8._____ Leads should emphasize a story's magnitude as well as its local and unusual details.

9._____ Every lead must be attributed.

10.____ A blind lead reports only a story's topic, not its substance.

11.____ Journalists have abandoned the practice of localizing and updating their leads.

12.____ Leads, like headlines, use the present tense and eliminate the articles: "a," "an" and "the."

13.____ A "label lead" fails to emphasize the news: a story's action or consequences.

14.____ A good lead often begins with the time and place that a story occurred.

15.____ Summary leads usually tell stories in chronological order, beginning with their topics' earliest developments.

16.____ For variation, a good lead often begins with a long clause or phrase.

17.____ The best leads are general, saving a story's specific details for the following paragraphs.

18.____ While writing leads, journalists prefer the active voice and normal word order: subject, verb and direct object.

Chapter 7. Alternative Leads

True/False Questions

Name:_____

1._____   An alternative lead is called a "nut graf."

2._____   Stories with a delayed lead cannot use a nut graf.

3._____   An alternative lead may continue for three or four paragraphs.

4._____   Alternative leads can use quotations or descriptions, but not anecdotes.

5._____   Alternative leads are also called "suitcase leads."

6._____   Critics charge that alternative leads fail to emphasize stories' most important details.

7._____   The best quotations for a lead will emphasize a startling detail rather than try to summarize an entire story.

8._____   Question leads are most appropriate for light, humorous — not serious — news stories.

9._____   "Soft leads," like traditional summaries, eliminate the possibility of surprise in a news story.

10._____   The "nut graf" usually appears at the end of a story.

11._____   "Jello-O journalism" refers to the continued use of routine summary leads.

12._____   The "nut graf" should contain an anecdote, quotation or description.

13._____   The quotations used in leads should be brief and self-explanatory.

14._____   Entire stories, including their leads, can be told in chronological order.

15._____   Journalists can use either a full or a partial quotation in leads.

Chapter 8. The Body of a News Story

True/False Questions

Name:_____

1.____ The inverted-pyramid style presents facts in chronological order.

2.____ Stories written in the focus style always begin with a summary lead..

3.____ The second paragraph in a news story using the inverted-pyramid style normally presents all the necessary background information.

4.____ Every item in a list should be in parallel form.

5.____ The term "leapfrogging" refers to stories that present facts in descending order of importance.

6.____ News stories told in the inverted-pyramid style usually end with their least important details — not with any type of summary or conclusion.

7.____ A transition can repeat a key word, idea or phrase used in the previous paragraph.

8.____ A good transition often summarizes the topic it introduces, revealing whatever was said or done about it.

9.____ Like leads, transitional sentences can take the form of questions.

10.____ The hourglass style works well with stories about events that have meaningful chronologies.

11.____ The details within each paragraph should be reported in chronological order even when the overall story is not reported in chronological order.

12.____ Reporters find lists effective only when placed in their stories' final paragraphs.

13.____ Stories that use the inverted-pyramid style are difficult to trim.

14.____ Every sentence in a news story should be short and simple.

15.____ If a story contains several major subtopics, reporters usually try to mention all the topics in their opening paragraphs.

16.____ When shifting to a new topic, it is often wise to report that the topic was "introduced" or "discussed," then proceed to more specific details about the topic.

17.____ The body of an inverted-pyramid story normally presents facts in descending order of importance.

Chapter 9. Quotations and Attribution

True/False Questions

Name:_____

1._____   Reporters using indirect quotations can rewrite and improve a source's wording.

2._____   The placement of quotation marks around one or two words used in an ordinary way is called an orphan quote.

3._____   Reporters often put the verb of attribution before the name of the source, just for variety.

4._____   Words such as "said," "explained," "added" and "pointed out" can be used interchangeably while attributing direct quotations.

5._____   Both direct and indirect quotations should be placed inside quotation marks.

6._____   Many journalists believe anonymous sources undermine the credibility of the news.

7._____   Reporters often summarize a major point then, for emphasis, use a direct quotation that repeats the point.

8._____   Verbs such as "hope," "feel," "think" and "believe" are acceptable as words of attribution.

9._____   When sources give reporters information on background, the reporters may quote the sources directly but not use their names or exact titles.

10.____   Reporters must attribute all undisputed facts but not statements of opinion.

11.____   The attribution should be placed near the end, not beginning, of a long quotation.

12.____   Any quotation is acceptable for a news story, so long as it is the speaker's exact words.

13.____   Good stories often use one long quotation after another.

14.____   Direct quotations should be attributed only once, no matter how long they are.

15.____   All reporters agree that they should never alter direct quotations, even to correct grammatical mistakes.

16.____   Reporters can paraphrase direct quotations but cannot place quotation marks around statements they paraphrase.

Chapter 10. Interviews

True/False Questions

Name:_____

1._____ Reporters seek to interview the best available sources, meaning those who are knowledgeable, articulate and accessible.

2._____ To save time, reporters often interview sources in newsrooms or at luncheon meetings.

3._____ Reporters normally try to begin an interview by asking their most difficult question.

4._____ If there is enough time, reporters will try to show a story to their source before the story's publication so the source can check its accuracy.

5._____ Reporters interviewing sources for a feature story, such as a personality profile, need the same information as ones interviewing for a news story, plus descriptions of the subject's environment, mannerisms, appearance and other picturesque details.

6._____ Newspaper reporters use tape recorders while conducting most interviews.

7._____ Closed-end questions are the best ones for reporters to ask.

8._____ Reporters rarely research a subject before conducting an interview so they can remain unbiased.

9._____ Although many state laws allow journalists to tape record interviews without informing their sources, the ethical practice is to tell the source.

10._____ Newspapers report most in-depth interviews in a question-and-answer format.

11._____ No matter what kind of story reporters are investigating, they usually interview only two or three sources.

12._____ Reporters ask questions relevant to what they expect will be the central point of their stories.

13._____ If a source is reluctant to talk about a topic, reporters should try to intimidate the source into answering their questions.

Chapter 11. Writing Obituaries

True/False Questions

Name:_____

1._____ Obituaries are one of the least popular sections in newspapers.

2._____ Obituaries are probably the most closely read stories in newspapers.

3._____ Newspapers usually devote large amounts of resources to obituaries.

4._____ Obituaries usually announce a person's death, describe the person's life and family and summarize funeral arrangements.

5._____ It is important for an obituary to contain the exact address of the deceased.

6._____ Obituary writers try to include eulogies and euphemisms.

7._____ The lead for a good obituary simply reports the person's age, address and time and cause of death.

8._____ Obituaries are news stories.

9._____ All obituaries include the cause of death.

10._____ Jim Nicholson, the obituary writer for the Philadelphia Daily News, is famous because he writes richly detailed obituaries about ordinary people.

11._____ A good obituary is written in chronological order, beginning with a person's birth, education and marriage.

12._____ Obituaries are funeral notices.

13._____ Obituaries seem detached and unfeeling because reporters rarely take the time to go into depth.

14._____ Obituaries emphasize death, not life.

15._____ Even on the day a celebrity dies, reporters may recall anecdotes that will make readers laugh.

121

Chapter 12. Speeches and Meetings

True/False Questions

Name:_____

1._____ Most news organizations cover only the most newsworthy of the speeches and meetings that happen in their cities.

2._____ The lead for an advance story should simply identify the group that has scheduled a speech or meeting, then report the event's time and location.

3._____ Advance stories are usually longer than follow stories.

4._____ The reporters writing a follow story should present information in the order of its importance, not the order in which it arose during a speech or meeting.

5._____ If a story involves several major topics, reporters should try to summarize all those topics in their stories' opening paragraphs.

6._____ To save space at the end of a story, reporters can simply mention that a speaker or group "discussed" or "considered" several less important topics.

7._____ A good transition will report that a speaker or group "turned to another topic."

8._____ Follow stories should not repeat any of the details reported in advance stories.

9._____ After writing their leads, reporters can use a list to introduce their stories' most important subtopics.

10._____ An ideal lead for a follow story about a speech or meeting will report that a specific topic was "considered" or "discussed."

11._____ Reporters never pay any attention to meeting agendas or advance copies of speeches.

12._____ When a speaker attacks another person, the reporter should include in the story a response from the target of the attack.

13._____ Reporters try to insert colorful details—such as a speaker's mannerisms or a crowd's reaction—in their speech or meeting stories.

14._____ It's OK to start every paragraph of a speech story with the attribution to the speaker.

Chapter 13. Specialized Types of Stories

True/False Questions

Name _____

1. _____   Sidebar stories are opportunities for reporters to editorialize and comment on news events.

2. _____   Brights that have a surprise ending often use a suspended-interest lead instead of a summary lead.

3. _____   The best way to organize a roundup story is by source, so that all facts and quotations from a particular source are kept together.

4. _____   The lead for a follow-up story usually recapitulates the original news event.

5. _____   Editors and producers dislike brights and consider them a waste of space and time.

6. _____   Media critics have complained that news organizations fail to follow stories to their conclusion.

7. _____   A common example of the roundup story is one that summarizes several traffic accidents that occurred since the last publication.

8. _____   News organizations try to avoid follow-up stories until they have a number of new developments to report.

Chapter 14. Feature Stories

True/False Questions

Name:_____

1._____ Features describe recent events, such as meetings, crimes and accidents.

2._____ The most important information in a feature story is presented first, the details last.

3._____ Features also are called human interest stories.

4._____ Reporters follow a formula to write feature stories.

5._____ It is acceptable to publish features that attract a small audience.

6._____ Reporters' personal experiences should never influence their choice of feature story topics.

7._____ Profiles summarize a person's entire life.

8._____ Compared to news stories, features use more color, description, quotations and anecdotes.

9._____ Feature writers looking for a good topic can use the concept of "universal needs."

10._____ Historical features during the impeachment of Bill Clinton included stories about the impeachment of Andrew Johnson in 1868.

11._____ Feature stories should be factual, fair, balanced and original—not fiction.

12._____ Feature writers can use techniques from drama and fiction: characterization, setting, conflict, time, dialogue and narrative.

13._____ Explanatory features also are called "local situation" or "interpretive" features or "sidebars."

14._____ Journalists should avoid collectors and craft enthusiasts as subjects for feature stories.

15._____ Features should be objective.

Chapter 15. Public Affairs Reporting

True/False Questions

Name:_____

1._____ "Discovery" is the process in which attorneys exchange information before a trial.

2._____ Police officers often view news reporters with suspicion, while reporters think of police officers as tight-lipped and secretive.

3._____ Criminal and civil trials are always open to reporters, but the jury selection process never is.

4._____ Reporters can inspect all records of public school students and personnel.

5._____ Reporters like to rely on information they get from police department public information officer and rarely bother going to the scenes of crimes and accidents.

6._____ Criminal history information is public record in most states but law enforcement authorities are reluctant to release it because it might jeopardize a suspect's right to a fair trial.

7._____ Young reporters often have the police beat as their first assignment because it is one of the easiest jobs in the newsroom.

8._____ One obstacle to thorough coverage of local government is that small numbers of public affairs reporters often must cover many governmental units.

9._____ City governments tend to be more professional than county governments, but city governments also are less open to the press and public.

10._____ The federal court system and the court systems of most states have three tiers.

11._____ Cities, counties and public school districts get most of their money from local income taxes.

12._____ The police blotter and the incident report both contain basic information about crimes but the incident report provides more details.

13._____ In most states, a person can be tried for a crime only after being indicted by a grand jury, but the federal government has abandoned the use of grand juries.

14._____ A criminal trial begins with the selection of the citizens who will serve on the jury.

15._____ Reporters often try to explain changes in property tax rates by showing how the tax owed on a typical home will change.

16._____ The coverage of civil cases has become more difficult in recent years because attorneys have routinely sought and judges have granted orders sealing many court records.

17._____ Real estate assessment records reveal the owner, legal description and assessed value for all land and buildings in a county.

Chapter 16. Understanding and Using the Internet

True/False Questions

Name:_____

1._____ The Internet and the World Wide Web are the same thing.

2._____ Gopher was the first browser to automate different log-in procedures and retrieve information to a user's computer.

3._____ Journalists do not use the Internet for factual information because it is not reliable.

4._____ Because of time spent on the Internet, journalists write fewer stories.

5._____ E-mails are just as good as personal interviews.

6._____ Reporters do not always know who is responding to their e-mails.

7._____ Many reporters use browser bookmarks much as they use address books.

8._____ Advanced searching on search engines can narrow the number of helpful URLs considerably.

9._____ Search engines are the same; the difference is in their advertising and marketing.

10._____ Implied Boolean logic uses a space in place of the keyword connector "or."

11._____ Newsgroup messages are sent to e-mail addresses.

12._____ Mailing lists and newsgroups are similar to online discussions

13._____ Reporters should be careful when using information from the Internet.

14._____ The Internet is a convenient reporting tool.

15._____ The Internet cannot replace good reporting procedures.

Chapter 17. Advanced Reporting

True/False Questions

Name:_____

1._____   Reporters deal with many forms of statistical information almost daily.

2._____   Stories explaining statistical information never emphasize the story's human interest angle.

3._____   Reporters who include statistics in their stories should present them as simply as possible.

4._____   Informal polls enable news organizations to describe accurately the sentiment of the entire community on any issue.

5._____   The lead of an informal poll story should include the opinions of everyone who was polled.

6._____   Poll stories should identify every person quoted.

7._____   In a poll story, if one person is quoted, every person interviewed in the story should be quoted.

8._____   Reporters should analyze for readers respondents' answers to poll questions by labeling the answers as "interesting," "thoughtful" or "uninformed."

9._____   Computers have become an important technological tool to help reporters gather and analyze information, write and edit their stories, and design pages.

10._____   A city directory is an example of a database.

11._____   Only large national or regional newspapers can afford to employ computer-assisted reporting techniques because of the cost and complexity of such projects.

12._____   Computer-assisted reporting can replace old-fashioned reporting because of the amount of information it gathers.

Chapter 18. Writing for Broadcast

True/False Questions

Name:_____

1._____ People listen to broadcast news to find out detailed information.

2._____ The broadcast and print media are different; therefore, the types of stories chosen for each are different.

3._____ Broadcast journalists must think in terms of listeners' ability to remember what is being said.

4._____ Broadcast journalists do not use contractions.

5._____ Saying "today" or "tomorrow' within a newscast is ambiguous.

6._____ Broadcast journalists make a story as readable as possible so it can be announced by someone else.

7._____ Long sentences combining several ideas are ideal for broadcast.

8._____ About 25 lines make up one minute of air time.

9._____ Transitions smooth the movement from one story to another.

10._____ Broadcast journalists spell out numbers up to and including eleven.

11._____ The soft lead is called a throwaway lead.

12._____ Broadcast stories reflect the inverted-pyramid model.

13._____ Datelines are omitted in broadcast writing.

14._____ Verbs often are in the present tense.

15._____ Broadcast writers circle all parts of the copy that are not to be read by the announcer.

Chapter 19. The News Media and the PR Practitioner

True/False Questions

Name:_____

1._____ It is important to use a client's name several times in a news release so that journalists will be sure to use the client's name in the story.

2._____ To get their news releases published, public relations practitioners must think and write like journalists.

3._____ Practitioners' news releases must serve the needs of the public and the client to get their client's name in the news.

4._____ Few news stories have public relations origins.

5._____ Most editors prefer to receive a news release several days or weeks in advance of the event.

6._____ Practitioners use AP style for news releases sent to newspapers and broadcast style for news releases sent to broadcast stations.

7._____ Practitioners do not worry about proofreading their news releases because an editor will review the news release anyway.

8._____ Reporters' No. 1 reason for rejecting news releases is that many of the releases are poorly written.

9._____ Journalists are more likely to use a news release about a genuine event than one about a contrived event, such as a ribbon-cutting, ground-breaking or gavel-passing.

10._____ While rewriting news releases, journalists eliminate laudatory adjectives, puffery, gush, platitudes and self-praise.

11._____ Whenever possible, reporters localize news releases.

12._____ A good news release will urge the public to act.

13._____ After deciding to use a news release, journalists rarely bother to edit or rewrite it.

14._____ Few news releases present both sides of a controversial issue.

Chapter 20. Communication Law

True/False Questions

Name:_____

1._____   The right of the press and public to attend judicial proceedings can never be abridged.

2._____   The federal government and all state governments have laws that open public meetings and records, but the laws contain many exemptions.

3._____   Under modern libel law, plaintiffs must prove the falsity of the defamatory statements.

4._____   Private individuals who sue for libel must prove negligence, which may include failure to check public records, misspelling or confusing names, or transposing dates and figures.

5._____   Journalists have an absolute right of access to crime, accident or disaster scenes.

6._____   All government workers are public officials for purposes of a libel suit.

7._____   News organizations always escape liability for defamatory statements if they prove they accurately quoted defamatory charges made by other people.

8._____   Modern courts usually treat broadcast defamation as libel, not slander.

9._____   Information drawn from public records, such as property tax information or court documents, can never be the basis for a lawsuit over publicity to private facts.

10._____   Such things as interviewing acquaintances and examining public records do not constitute intrusion on a person's privacy.

11._____   Defamatory statements are those that lower a person's reputation in the community or deter others from associating or doing business with that person.

12._____   Public figures must prove that defamatory statements were with ill will.

13._____   The plaintiff in a false light privacy lawsuit does not have to prove injury to reputation.

14._____   For purposes of a libel suit, publication means only that the defamatory statement was made to someone other than the person defamed.

15._____   Statements of opinion may be protected from libel suits, so long as they cannot be understood as stating actual facts about the plaintiff.

16._____   The U.S. Supreme Court has said reporters cannot be subpoenaed by courts or grand juries to testify about confidential sources and information.

17._____   The qualified privilege defense protects news organizations when they report defamatory statements made in governmental proceedings or records.

Chapter 21. Ethics

True/False Questions

Name:_____

1._____   Deciding whom to quote in a story is a value judgment.

2._____   Being ethical means being able to distinguish between right and wrong.

3._____   Only 11 percent of the public believe "almost all" of what media report.

4._____   Two important questions to ask when facing ethical decisions are "Who will be hurt, and how many?" and "Who will be helped, and how many?"

5._____   The micro issue is the main reason for publishing or airing a story.

6._____   Good journalists no longer have biases.

7._____   About 47 percent of U.S. citizens believe the media do not care about the people they report on.

8._____   News stories often are the sources of a second wound to victims.

9._____   It is now acceptable to publish the names of all juvenile defenders.

10._____   Gossip is a good source for news topics.

11._____   Managing editors encourage their journalists to become involved in city politics.

12._____   Professional organizations require members to follow their ethics codes.

13._____   Good journalists are also compassionate journalists.

14._____   A question to ask when making an ethical decision is, "Does this decision fit the kind of journalism I believe in and the way people should treat one another?"

Chapter 22. Careers in Journalism

True/False Questions

Name:_____

1._____ Salaries in journalism have never been higher or jobs as plentiful.

2._____ Being able to write well is an advantage in the journalism industry only.

3._____ Talented writers are also good grammarians, who can spell and write clearly and accurately.

4._____ About 75 percent of new journalism professionals come from college journalism programs.

5._____ Journalism students do not need to obtain experience while still in school to get a job.

6._____ Small news organizations offer journalists a variety of assignments.

7._____ Successful applicants appear for a job interview wearing jeans.

8._____ Applicants invited to a job interview are not expected to ask questions.

9._____ Applicants should research the media organization before the interview.

10._____ Journalists with new technology skills have lower salaries than the average reporter.

11._____ Beats involve specific topics that are especially newsworthy to the public.

12._____ The percentage of minorities that newsrooms employ now exceeds that of minorities in the U.S. population.

13._____ Job applicants should include short explanations with their work samples, describing what they did.

14._____ Beginning journalists never work overtime or on the weekends.

Answers for True/False Questions

Chapter 1	Chapter 2	Chapter 3	Chapter 4	Chapter 5
1. False	1. False	1. False	1. False	1. True
2. True	2. True	2. False	2. True	2. False
3. False	3. True	3. True	3. False	3. True
4. False	4. False	4. False	4. False	4. True
5. True	5. False	5. True	5. False	5. False
6. False	6. True	6. True	6. True	6. False
7. False	7. True	7. False	7. False	7. False
8. True	8. False	8. False	8. True	8. False
9. True	9. True	9. False	9. False	9. True
10. False	10. True	10. True	10. True	10. True
11. False	11. True	11. False	11. False	11. True
12. True	12. False	12. False	12. True	12. False
13. True	13. True	13. False	13. False	13. False
14. False	14. False	14. False	14. True	
15. True	15. True	15. True	15. False	

Chapter 6	Chapter 7	Chapter 8	Chapter 9	Chapter 10
1. False	1. False	1. False	1. True	1. True
2. False	2. False	2. False	2. True	2. False
3. True	3. True	3. False	3. False	3. False
4. False	4. False	4. True	4. False	4. False
5. True	5. False	5. False	5. False	5. True
6. False	6. True	6. True	6. True	6. False
7. False	7. False	7. True	7. False	7. False
8. True	8. True	8. True	8. False	8. False
9. False	9. False	9. True	9. True	9. True
10. False	10. False	10. True	10. False	10. False
11. False	11. False	11. False	11. False	11. False
12. False	12. False	12. False	12. False	12. True
13. True	13. True	13. False	13. False	13. False
14. False	14. True	14. False	14. True	
15. False	15. True	15. True	15. False	
16. False		16. False	16. True	
17. False		17. True		
18. True				

Chapter 11
1. False
2. True
3. False
4. True
5. False
6. False
7. False
8. False
9. False
10. True
11. False
12. False
13. True
14. False
15. True

Chapter 12
1. True
2. False
3. False
4. True
5. True
6. False
7. False
8. False
9. True
10. False
11. False
12. True
13. True
14. False

Chapter 13
1. False
2. True
3. False
4. False
5. False
6. True
7. True
8. False

Chapter 14
1. False
2. False
3. True
4. False
5. False
6. False
7. False
8. True
9. True
10. True
11. True
12. True
13. True
14. False
15. True

Chapter 15
1. True
2. True
3. False
4. False
5. False
6. True
7. False
8. True
9. True
10. True
11. False
12. True
13. False
14. True
15. True
16. True
17. True

Chapter 16
1. False
2. True
3. False
4. False
5. False
6. True
7. True
8. True
9. False
10. True
11. False
12. True
13. True
14. True
15. True

Chapter 17
1. True
2. False
3. True
4. False
5. False
6. True
7. False
8. False
9. True
10. True
11. False
12. False

Chapter 18
1. False
2. False
3. True
4. False
5. False
6. True
7. False
8. False
9. True
10. True
11. False
12. False
13. True
14. True
15. True

Chapter 19
1. False
2. True
3. True
4. False
5. False
6. True
7. False
8. False
9. True
10. True
11. True
12. False
13. False
14. True

Chapter 20
1. False
2. True
3. True
4. True
5. False
6. False
7. False
8. True
9. True
10. True
11. True
12. False
13. True
14. True
15. True
16. False
17. True

Chapter 21	Chapter 22
1. True	1. True
2. True	2. False
3. True	3. True
4. True	4. True
5. False	5. False
6. False	6. True
7. True	7. False
8. True	8. False
9. False	9. True
10. False	10. False
11. False	11. True
12. False	12. False
13. True	13. True
14. True	14. False